THE VICTORIANS
AND EDWARDIANS
AT PLAY

John Hannavy

First published in Great Britain in 2009 by Shire Publications Ltd,
Midland House, West Way, Botley, Oxford OX2 0PH, United Kingdom.
443 Park Avenue South, New York, NY 10016, USA.

E-mail: shire@shirebooks.co.uk   .   www.shirebooks.co.uk

A CIP catalogue record for this book is available from the British Library.

Shire Library no. 550   .   ISBN-13: 978 0 7478 0720 9

John Hannavy has asserted his right under the Copyright, Designs and Patents Act, 1988, to be identified as the author of this book.

Printed in China through Worldprint Ltd.

09 10 11 12 13   10 9 8 7 6 5 4 3 2 1

COVER IMAGE
A camel ride at London Zoo, from a postcard c.1907.

TITLE PAGE IMAGE
The classic Edwardian seaside holiday postcard view – children paddling with their mothers at the water's edge on Llandudno beach in North Wales c.1908. Scenes like this were repeated around the entire coast and typify the Edwardians enjoying themselves – even if the children seem to be dressed in a strangely formal manner for such activities!

CONTENTS PAGE IMAGE
The tearooms at Birkenshaw Cottage, Rouken Glen, c.1908. Rouken Glen, four miles south of Glasgow City Centre, had been gifted to the city, and opened as a public park in 1906. The tearooms seen here are now a Chinese restaurant, the Cathay Cuisine.

The author's own website

Shire Publications is supporting the   on of trees.

CONTENTS

Preface 4
Introduction 5
In the Park 13
Dancing 17
Enjoying the Regatta 19
A Day at the Races 23
At the Zoo 27
Punch & Judy 31
Cricket 33
A Round of Golf 34
Playing and Watching Football 39
Scouting 41
Pierrots & Minstrels 43
On the Beach 45
Tennis 52
Bowls 54
Winter Sports 56
Hunting 60
Shooting 62
Fishing 65
Listening to the Band 67
Pleasure Beaches 68
All the Fun of the Fair 71
A Summer Picnic 73

A Trip on a Pleasure Steamer 74
Promenading 79
Motoring 83
Pageants & Dressing Up 85
A Few Days in the Country 86
Cycling 89
Climbing & Mountaineering 90
Sports Day 93
A Nice Cup of Tea 94
Visiting Exhibitions 97
Motor Racing 100
Playing Cards 101
Boating 103
Croquet 107
Children Playing 109
Courtship 111
Enjoying a Pint of Beer 112
A Walk in the Gardens 114
Roller Skating 117
Sightseeing 118
Shopping 120
A Life on the Ocean Wave 122
Holidaying Abroad 125
Index 128

PREFACE

The idea of compiling a book about how the Victorians and Edwardians spent their leisure time has been with me for several years, and it is especially pleasing to see it come to fruition. With its companion volume *The Victorians and Edwardians at Work*, it celebrates a period when first the photographic print, and later the picture postcard, were the media through which British life was defined and celebrated.

As with every book I have produced over the past thirty-five years, although it is my name on the cover, the project is not the work of just the author. It depends for its interest on the knowledge and input of many local historians and collectors who have added that little bit of context and colour to the story each of these images has to tell us. Once again, my own collection of Victorian and Edwardian images – built up over almost forty years of searching auction houses, flea-markets, antique shops and junk shops – is the source of the majority of the pictures.

I owe a growing debt of gratitude to the friends and dealers who continue to bring exceptional images and collections of pictures to my notice, and to the many people who have answered my questions about the images you see on these pages. It is the information in the text and captions that really brings these pictures to life, and that has been generously shared by the many collectors and historians whose expertise has expanded my own knowledge.

Colour is the great thing in so many of these pictures – we are so used to seeing the past through monochrome or sepia photographs, that to experience the Victorian and Edwardian world brought to life in many of these remarkable tinted images, seems somehow to bring us a little closer to that world.

John Hannavy, Great Cheverell, 2008

A group of children walking and playing on the Fish Quay at Blyth, Northumberland, c.1900. Typical of children of the period, despite the fact that they seem to be dressed in their 'Sunday best', all but one of the girls are barefoot.

This 1/6th plate ambrotype – a direct positive image on glass – was taken by an unknown itinerant beach photographer in the 1860s or early 1870s. Travelling photographers used cameras with internal processing – which meant that the picture could be developed in a tray of chemicals at the bottom of the camera, the plate being manipulated by the photographer through light-tight arm holes. Such cameras meant that the photographer could travel and work anywhere without needing all the paraphernalia of a portable darkroom or darktent.

INTRODUCTION

The whole idea of leisure time and leisure pastimes was, for the majority of people at least, a hard-won privilege unheard of before the nineteenth-century reforms of employment rights. Hitherto, such indulgences were the exclusive domain of the wealthy. Even photography itself was originally practised only by those with unlimited time and a deep purse – the first amateurs to travel with their cameras were land-owners, doctors, lawyers and the like.

It would be late in the Victorian era before the masses could afford to visit a photographer, and the early twentieth century (the box camera revolution) before they could afford to create their own mementoes of their leisure time, their holidays and their sporting enthusiasms.

Ironically, even the humble peasant had enjoyed more free time to pursue simple pleasures in medieval Britain than was available to the majority of workers at the beginning of the

A young girl looks across the 'serpentine lake' in Wigan's Mesnes (or Meynes) Park in 1905, towards a group of youths standing at the foot of the steps leading to the pavilion. Parks like this (Mesnes Park was created in 1877–8) were established in many towns throughout the country, funded partly by local authorities and partly by local mill, factory and colliery owners. In 1889 Wigan's showpiece park was described as 'one of the lungs of the town, a breathing spot for the thousands who, for most of their time, are cooped up in factories, collieries &c… and in the spring and summer, Meynes Park presents a pretty sight.'

Victorian era. As will be seen elsewhere in this book, laws were passed in the fifteenth century to try and curtail the amount of time archers were spending playing golf. Four centuries later, the vast majority of people had neither the time nor the money for such indulgences!

With no money to travel, and with limited free time anyway, the local park became a key component of the lives of working people. Local authorities, often prompted by generous endowments from local employers and landowners, developed beautiful municipal parks in most towns and cities, often with a pavilion, and invariably with a bandstand where local factory or church bands would perform on a Sunday afternoon.

All the parks had elaborate gardens, many had small serpentine lakes, and all were furnished with strategically positioned benches from which to enjoy the views.

Armies of gardeners and park attendants maintained and ruled these small patches of green in the midst of grim industrial urban areas. Their rules were published at the park gates, and those who ventured into their local parks understood and accepted that their demeanour and their behaviour had to conform. Walking or sitting in the park may have been a leisure activity, but it was still subject to accepted standards and disciplines.

One of the first 'crazes' of the photographic era was collecting and viewing 3D or stereoscopic images. From the late 1850s, every Victorian drawing room had a stereoscopic viewer – some of them simple hand-held devices, others elaborate pieces of furniture. New stereocards were published weekly, and were available through local print-sellers and photographic studios. The *Stereoscopic Magazine* in the early 1860s brought some remarkable 3D images to the notice of the public, albeit at a price that placed them beyond the budget of many. The London Stereoscopic and Photographic Company published hundreds of cards, many of them in large sets, covering subjects that ranged from educational – views of different parts of the world being very popular – to pure entertainment.

Genre cards included subjects ranging from historical re-enactments to humorous situations such as party games. Many of these images were later cropped down to the carte-de-visite size print, which became the ubiquitous format of the 1860s and fitted the standard Victorian family album.

Lantern slide lectures were another popular entertainment. Village halls, church halls and assorted other locations were filled with people keen to hear stories from intrepid travellers who had journeyed to far-flung corners of the world.

For the really affluent, sets of slides in beautiful fitted wooden boxes could be purchased, complete with accompanying scripts, so that the lectures could even be delivered by those who had perhaps never been out of their own town!

There was a commonly held view amongst those Victorians who pioneered the great exhibitions that punctuated the second half of the century, that leisure time – in part at least – should be instructive. The Great Exhibition at the Crystal Palace in 1851 set a pattern of combining commerce with instruction, and people in their millions paid to pass through the turnstiles. Halls devoted to the art, culture and industry of different parts of the world were the popular attractions of the Great Exhibition, where visitors could learn something of the cultures of foreign lands – the sort of instructive entertainment we now get from television

'Caught at Last', one of a series of humorous stereoscopic genre cards from the late 1850s on the subject of party games. These cards were individually hand-tinted with coloured dyes by teams of women, each of whom might be responsible for only one of the colours. Five or six different colours have been used on this card, with the sepia colour of the albumen print providing the background.

and from lavishly illustrated 'coffee-table' books. The Egyptian Court was a particular favourite, dominated by giant 'mummy' cases, a sphinx and palm trees.

When the Crystal Palace was dismantled and moved from its original site in Hyde Park to that part of Sydenham which bears its name to this day, the instructional and educational aspect was maintained, albeit with some less demanding entertainment added.

At around the same time, art schools started to open, offering the artisan and the craftsman the chance to take classes in a growing range of creative subjects.

By the early years of the twentieth century, exhibition sites had to offer more – and the huge White City complex in London combined exhibition halls with a sports stadium and a number of purely recreational rides and experiences. The 'Flip Flap' was the most dramatic of the rides, while the scenic railway was probably the most popular.

Exhibitions fired an enthusiasm, at least amongst those who could afford it, for travel. For even the relatively well educated and well off, the chance to travel and to explore and experience other parts of Britain – let alone foreign countries – was a possibility only opened up in the mid nineteenth century, when statutory holidays were introduced at about the same time as the major railway expansion.

Right: The 'Flip-Flap' was one of the most popular attractions at the Franco-British Exhibition, held in 1908 at the newly constructed White City complex in London. The site had been developed primarily for exhibitions, but a stadium was added to the plans when London took over the hosting of the 1908 Olympics from Rome.

Above opposite: This postcard, 'Watching the Boats at Fleetwood', was published in 1908. Above the ladies' heads can be seen the twin funnels of the Londonderry steamer at the quayside.

The curiosity for experiencing travel to other parts of the country, and to other lands, is what brought Thomas Cook into the travel business – his first party of temperance travellers journeyed from Leicester to the Trossachs region of Scotland in the 1840s. It is interesting to note that Cook's first package tour was for a working-class party and not the well off. These were people who had probably never seen the open countryside before!

By the mid 1850s, he was offering package trips to the Exposition Universelle in Paris – although the package-tour innovator had significantly failed to negotiate a cheap rate with the ferry owners on the channel.

The pictures in this book are drawn predominantly from the picture postcard – which in the Edwardian era was rather like the text message or email of today. It was a cheap, simple and reliable way of keeping in regular contact in the years before the telephone became commonplace in people's homes. Thanks to a super-efficient postal service, postcards could be slipped into the postbox first thing in the morning with delivery locally almost guaranteed by lunchtime. In major towns and cities, there were half a dozen collections and deliveries a day, so it was possible to make arrangements by postcard to meet someone that same evening. As the popularity of this means of making contact increased, of course, it generated an enormous demand for the cards themselves.

The photographic postcard started to appear in the early years of the twentieth century, and for the first few years all cards had a little white strip along the bottom of the picture for a brief message – postal regulations permitted only the address to be on the reverse. Those restrictive rules were changed in 1902, and from then onwards the split-back card we still recognise today came into everyday use. That opened up the possibility of sending longer messages, further increasing the medium's popularity, and by the middle of the century's first decade, postcards were being bought, written and sold in their millions. Of course, as demand for picture postcards increased, so did demand for more varied photographs. It would appear that by 1905, just about every possible subject was considered saleable.

Postcard collecting was already an established hobby before the end of the nineteenth century, so as new card designs and themes were marketed, they were bought by collectors as well as by those wishing to send messages to friends. Subjects ranged from those we would still recognise today – famous buildings, landscapes and famous people – through to those cards that hold the greatest fascination for us today.

Some time around the turn of the twentieth century – 1903 or 1904 – innovative photographers and publishers introduced series of cards which celebrated the diversity of working life in Britain and, alongside the already established range of scenic views, these were quickly joined by cards depicting leisure pursuits as well. In many cases they were photographed and published locally – depicting local people at work and play. The photographs would be taken by a local photographer, providing a small but welcome additional source of income, and the fact that every aspect of the process was handled by local people who knew and understood the local lifestyle gives these postcards considerable importance as social history documents.

Children of all walks of life love dressing up! In 1854, Roger Fenton took this photograph of the Prince of Wales, later King Edward VII, dressed as 'Winter', with Princess Louise.

The photographer's studio was a popular haunt for many holidaymakers. In the Victorian and Edwardian era, anything American was believed to be particularly exciting, so many seaside studios advertised themselves as producing 'American portraits' to give their work that special appeal!

It is hard for us to imagine today just how huge the impact of the photographic postcard was in this period, and perhaps even harder to imagine people today willingly posing for studies to be used in picture postcards. With very few exceptions, today's postcard subjects are bland and have an impersonal timelessness, which of course ensures that they have a long shelf life. This reflects the relegation of the postcard solely to the role of tourist memento, the communication aspect having long since been taken over by other, faster media.

For the people who posed for these pictures, a small measure of local celebrity was assured for the lifetime of the postcard, and it must have been quite an attractive proposition to use cards that carried photographs of yourself or your friends. This was an inspired piece of local marketing, probably ensuring larger than usual sales. The photographers and publishers who created the cards, however, cannot have dreamed of the importance their enterprises would have a hundred years later in defining what life was like in the early years of the twentieth century.

Many of the cards were printed in colour, crude colouring being created by multiple chromolithographic printings, giving an added realism and appeal to the images. Few local printing works could handle such sophistication, so while black-and-white versions of popular local cards were printed locally, many of the finest coloured examples of the same pictures were printed in Saxony.

That gives some idea of the scale of production – it would not have been worthwhile going to the trouble of colourising the images and having them printed abroad if print runs were small – and it is a reflection on the fleeting and immediate nature of the postcard message that so few of them were saved for posterity.

After the First World War, the world was a very different place, the social order started to change, and the increasing availability of low-priced cameras changed the nature of the photograph from being something everyone bought, to something almost everyone made.

An itinerant photographer on Blackpool beach captured this study of three small children in their donkey cart in August 1882. Compared with children seen in many Victorian and Edwardian photographs, these children have the much more casual dress we would normally associate with holidays, perhaps reflecting their social status. Blackpool was, after all, proud to proclaim itself the holiday resort of choice for the working class – the mill, factory and mine workers of the industrial northwest, where wages were low, holidays were without pay, and for many a single day at the seaside was considered luxury indeed.

With the increasing popularity of the telephone, the picture postcard moved from being an essential means of communication to something approaching the 'wish you were here' role it retains to this day. The range of subjects reduced dramatically, and thus the postcard's ability to reflect its age diminished. The window through which these early images let us look was not open for long!

Three ladies putting the world to rights on a park bench in the 1870s, location and photographer unknown. The lady on the left is crocheting, her yarn trailing on the ground beside her. This 1/6th plate ambrotype was taken by an itinerant photographer.

IN THE PARK

In these days when parks are crammed with signs telling people to keep off the grass, and not to play ball games, and when children are told to keep well away from water, it is good to remember that a century ago the local municipal park was a place where everyone could enjoy themselves in safety, where boating, playing ball games, and simply walking, co-existed happily with the business of just relaxing in the sunshine. Indeed, parks had been set up in Victorian times to offer the one thing they seem not to today – freedom to have fun! Teams of gardeners were employed to look after the every need of their oasis of green, tending beautifully kept flower beds, and competing with parks in neighbouring towns for the best floral displays. Parks had pavilions, bandstands and tearooms, and really were at the heart of the local community.

A policeman in a Brighton park (c.1906) appears to be rescuing a small dog from the attentions of an irate swan while elegantly dressed mothers and children look on – one of the more unusual postcards of Britain's parks!

The Children's Corner, in a park in Bournemouth, 1907. The park benches are filled with parents, aunts and uncles watching while their charges sail yachts or just play with sticks. The sender of this postcard, however, was elsewhere, sitting on the beach while her son Leslie was 'now in a deep hole in the sands with the water coming in over his boots and stockings.'

Children playing with model boats in the Round Pond in Kensington Gardens in the summer of 1906. In those days, parents were delighted to see their children's photographs published on postcards, and postcard publishers, ever keen to expand their ranges of cards, found children at play a very popular and commercially successful subject.

Children feeding the swans in Beveridge Park, Kirkcaldy, Fife. Produced in Saxony for Hartmann & Co, it was published in 1903. Just about every town had a similar card showing people enjoying the civic amenities.

Top: Dancing on the Central Pier, Blackpool c.1906. 'We have been dancing', wrote Edith in 1907 to her friend Maggie in Nottingham. 'We are enjoying ourselves very much.' Dancing on the pier was just one of many entertainments offered outdoors during the Edwardian summer – and it gave people the opportunity to enjoy themselves without paying to enter the town's major ballrooms. The sheer number of people enjoying themselves on the decking attests to the strength of the Central Pier, already fifty years old when this card was posted.

Above: 'Dancing – the Bottom Quadrille' was one of a number of stereos to take a lighthearted look at dancing. Both the stereo cards on these pages date from the late 1850s. Several publishers produced series like this.

Opposite: 'The Soirée' comes from a series of humorous cards produced by The London Stereoscopic & Photographic Company, which offered several different views of the pleasures of dancing. Each stereocard was tinted by hand so no two cards were ever exactly the same.

'Dancing on Spaniard's Road, Hampstead Heath', from a photograph taken c.1907. This sort of outdoor dancing was impromptu, and not necessarily always accompanied by music.

DANCING

During the Victorian and Edwardian years, formal dancing went from being an activity generally limited to private parties – and parties in affluent circles at that – to being a public entertainment that could be enjoyed in dance halls and ballrooms. The 1890s saw the working classes embrace dancing as a pastime, and, of course, as a way of making close contact with the opposite sex! To cater for demand, several late-Victorian music halls were built with flat floors to enable them to be used for dancing. Visiting public dance halls was, despite their popularity, initially considered a rather risqué activity because of their lack of supervision!

Development of dance halls was rapid. Blackpool's original Tower Pavilion dance hall opened in 1894 at the front of the tower complex, and the much larger Empress Ballroom opened as part of the Winter Gardens in 1896. The bigger, more luxurious and more famous Tower Ballroom opened a year later in 1897. The 3,000-capacity Locarno (later known as The Palace) followed in 1899.

By the end of the Edwardian era, most large towns and cities, and just about every holiday resort, offered dancing as one of the many entertainments available, but not everywhere welcomed them. When part of Southport's Winter Gardens was converted into a ballroom in 1897, the resort felt that this was taking the venue down-market!

Above: This colourful view of a rowing race entitled 'College Barges' was photographed in Oxford, but the card was posted in Glasgow in March 1909.

Below: Entitled 'The Race-Course, Henley on Thames', this view of the 1905 races was posted in Camberley in April 1906. Like so many Edwardian cards, the crowded boats are a reminder of life before modern, safety-conscious times.

Below opposite: 'The Morning of the Race, Lowestoft' shows the start of the major yacht race in the town's annual regatta in 1908, with a solitary little steamboat in amongst the yachts.

ENJOYING THE REGATTA

Rowing was highly popular in Victorian and Edwardian times both as a participative sport and as a spectator sport. According to Charles Dickens Jnr in his 1887 *Dickens's Dictionary of the Thames*, the Henley Rowing Club had been formed as early as 1830. Dickens also informed his readers that an annual Rowing Almanac was published at the offices of *The Field* and was 'edited by one of the best practical judges of rowing and matters aquatic in England.' As a testament to the popularity of the Henley Regatta, he devoted over seven pages in his book to the events, listing every cup-holder since the event was inaugurated. A single event for 1839 is listed, with the eight-man crew of 'First Trinity, Cambridge' picking up the Grand Challenge Cup. It would be fifteen years before they won it again. 'This, the most important gathering of amateur oarsmen in England', wrote Dickens, 'takes place usually about the beginning of July, and almost ranks with Ascot among the favourite fashionable meetings of the season.'

Success brought with it significant problems – the Victorians enjoying a few days out en masse caused real congestion. 'The river is so inconveniently crowded with steam launches, house boats, skiffs, gigs, punts, dingeys [sic], canoes, and every other conceivable and inconceivable variety of craft', wrote Dickens, 'that the racing boats have sometimes the greatest difficulty in threading a way through the crowd.'

Regattas were popular throughout the Victorian and Edwardian eras, and were held in many towns and villages throughout the country. While most river events focused on rowing, those held around the coast concentrated on yacht racing. All of them attracted large crowds, and for many of those attending the river regattas, living on houseboats for the duration of the event was all part of the adventure.

A group of onlookers standing on Henley Bridge while others, dressed in their ubiquitous black waistcoats and straw boaters, line the riverbank during the regatta in 1906. The decision to hold an annual regatta at Henley-on-Thames was taken at a meeting on 26 March 1839 at Henley Town Hall. Regular boat races were already established at Henley Reach and the formalising of the events was seen as a potentially significant

FREE LANDING

tourist attraction. The regatta has taken place almost every year since then – the only interruptions being the duration of the two world wars. What was a half-day event in 1839 now occupies five full days. In 1851, the year of the Great Exhibition at the Crystal Palace, Prince Albert added to his already busy schedule and agreed to become the first royal patron of the Regatta. Thereafter the event was known as 'Henley Royal Regatta'.

The grandstand at Ascot, packed to absolute capacity in 1904. The horses in this card look as though they have been added later by an artist – perhaps in the original photograph they were too blurred to be acceptable. They appear smaller than would be expected!

Taken during the 1903 St Leger meeting, this animated scene was captured as King Edward VII visited the course. The king was a regular visitor to the racetrack.

A DAY AT THE RACES

'Scarcely a week elapses in the racing or steeplechasing seasons without some opportunity being given the turfite for the pursuit of his favourite amusement', wrote Charles Dickens Jnr in the late 1880s. 'The most famous of the metropolitan racecourses is Epsom, with its time-honoured traditions of the Derby and Oaks; and one of the London weeks is the "Derby week", which is at the end of May or the beginning of June.' He also recorded his opinion that 'it is useful to remember that racecourse refreshments are almost always abominable, and that it is well to have as little to do with them as possible.'

Dickens never seems to have been reluctant to speak his mind, and, having bemoaned the high prices charged for access to the stands at both Epsom and Ascot in his *Dictionary of London 1888 – an Unconventional Handbook*, he warns would-be race-goers: 'There are, probably, even more welshers and thieves at the London race meetings than elsewhere, because the meetings, being more numerous and close at home, afford more constant employment to these industrious classes. The visitor who wants a wager should be very shy of depositing his money with anybody he does not know, and unless he is acquainted with a respectable bookmaker, ought to keep his money in his pocket. If not, he will most assuredly never see it again.' Wise advice, perhaps, even today! As these pictures show, the high prices did not discourage the race-goers one bit.

This view of the paddock and grandstand at Doncaster Racecourse, *c*.1909, shows the animated scene at the end of a race as the winner is led in. The card was one of a series supplied, according to the print on the back, 'free exclusively by Shurey's Publications', comprising 'Smart Novels', 'Yes or No' and 'Dainty Novels'. The sheer number of cards of the Doncaster meeting underlines the importance of the picture postcard during the Edwardian era. Doncaster's royal patronage no doubt contributed to its success.

Huge crowds at Doncaster races for the 1906 St Leger, published in 'The Wrench' postcard series. This card was posted in 1907.

Ascot Races were listed among *the* social events of the year, and detailed reports listing the rich and famous who turned out – and often what they wore as well – were carried in all the magazines that might be read by the upper echelons of English life. One correspondent, writing for the magazine *Chic* in 1904, described the scene in almost poetic terms, creating a word picture of the cream of Edwardian English society at play.

'The opening day of Ascot Races', he wrote, 'was the most brilliant that can be remembered. The lawns were crowded with a fluttering mass of beautifully gowned women and men in frock coats and top hats, and when the King and Queen arrived it would be difficult to imagine a more beautiful scene than was presented to the eye; the moving mass of human beings resolving itself into a veritable kaleidoscope of brilliant colour.'

The royal coach awaits the departure of King Edward VII from Doncaster races in 1903.

The horses approach the winning post during one of the races at the summer 1909 meeting at Chester racecourse.

In this 1905 view, entitled 'Epsom, the Winning Post' the photographer has chosen to take his picture from an unusual viewpoint, looking over the bookies' enclosure towards the stands. In so doing, he has offered us a rare view over the tented village and gypsy caravans, which were the temporary homes of the many people who congregated around the racecourse, running food and drink stalls, and the other amenities that added to the excitement of the event.

Below and bottom right: 'Elephant, 2d all the way', two of a long series of cards produced for London's Regents Park Zoo in the early years of the twentieth century. 'A ride not to be forgotten when we four meet again at the zoo. Love to yourself and Clumsy Dick', wrote Frances Hartford to her friend Lilian Trinder in Acton in 1905.

Bottom: 'Dromedary at the Zoo', another of the zoo's rides, photographed in 1905.

Following pages: Three girls set off on their camel ride while their mother and a younger brother look on. This beautiful tinted photograph of the camel ride at London Zoo was published c.1907.

AT THE ZOO

London's Regents Park Zoo is the oldest in the world. By the time Queen Victoria came to the throne, it had already been in existence for nine years – although not open to the public. Initially, it was conceived as a centre for the scientific study of animals – 'for teaching and elucidating zoology' – rather than as a form of entertainment, and was open only to members of the Zoological Society of London. All that changed in 1847 when the zoological gardens, facing financial collapse, had to find a way of making money and balancing the books. Opening the grounds to the public five days a week – keeping Sundays exclusively for the use of members – and charging them a shilling for the privilege of looking at the animals did the trick, and saved the zoo from closure.

The zoo had been the brainchild of Sir Stamford Raffles and others, but Raffles died before it was built. It initially drew its animals from the collection held in the Royal Menageries in the Tower of London, so the recently completed Regents Park was the ideal place to house it.

By the 1880s, visiting the zoo had become hugely popular. Many of the animals had been given names – Jumbo the six-ton Indian elephant being a particular favourite. Songs had been written about the pleasures of a day at the zoo, the visitor facilities on site had been praised for the quality of the experience, and prices had remained static for forty years.

In 1887, the price was still the same as it had been at the time of opening in 1847, and a one shilling adult ticket gained access to the entire site for a full day from 9am until sunset, except on certain holidays when it was reduced to a mere sixpence – the price always charged to children.

'The Gardens of the Zoological Society of London contain the largest and by far the best arranged collection of wild beasts, birds and reptiles in the world', wrote Charles Dickens Jnr

in 1887, 'and, being themselves laid out in the best taste and kept in the most perfect order, afford the best place of open-air amusement to be found in London.' The cab fare to reach the zoo from Charing Cross station was, he tells us, one shilling and sixpence.

Facilities were rather sophisticated by then, and Dickens recommended his readers to 'try the table d'hôte dinner' in the 'conveniently arranged refreshment room… [which] they can have served under the shade of the verandah, a very agreeable institution on a pleasant summer evening.' A shilling was still a large sum of money, so the zoo's visitors were probably largely drawn from the middle and upper classes. He went on to list the feeding times of the animals – from the pelicans at 2.30pm through to lions and tigers at 3pm and sea-lions half an hour later. He makes no mention of camel or elephant rides, which, if the postcards of the early twentieth century are anything to go by, became a highly popular attraction. At least fifty different postcard views of the zoo's many attractions were available by the end of the Edwardian era, and at least a dozen of them showed children riding the camels.

To become a member of the Zoological Society itself in the 1880s, a joining fee of £5 was required, and an annual subscription of £3, which included free admission tickets and other privileges.

The polar bear enclosure, London Zoo, c.1906. A zookeeper keeps an eye on the photographer, a little girl stares at the bear, while two women – one of them perhaps her mother – engage in conversation.

Codman's Punch & Judy Show, Lime Street, Liverpool, c.1909. A Punch & Judy Show had been presented regularly on this site for over forty years by the time this photograph was taken. The original Liverpool show was staged in 1868 by Richard Codman, but his son Richard Mortimer Codman had taken over in 1888. Due to redevelopment of the site, the show has moved from Lime Street, but the tradition is maintained to this day at Liverpool's Albert Dock.

PUNCH & JUDY

While Punch & Judy shows are often considered a traditional part of the Victorian and Edwardian seaside holiday, they thrived in towns and cities as well, and can be traced back to the seventeenth century. Travelling puppeteers regularly visited towns on their market days, offering entertainment with moral undertones!

Henry Mayhew, in his 1861 book *London Labour and the London Poor*, included a Punch & Judy script, and the detailed reminiscences of a puppeteer who claimed to be making £2 a day in 1860. 'The best pitch of all in London is Leicester Square', he told Mayhew, ' there's all sorts of classes there, you see, passing there. Then comes Regent Street (the corner of Burlington Street is uncommon good), and there's a good publican there besides. We don't do much in the city. People has their heads all full of business there, and them as is greedy arter the money, ain't no friend of Punch's.'

The puppeteers invariably referred to themselves as 'professors' and the best known was undoubtedly Richard Codman, whose original show in Llandudno started in 1860, pre-dating the famous Liverpool show by eight years. The Codman family still operates Punch & Judy shows in several locations, and prides itself in having been 'Established 150 years'.

CRICKET

Almost certainly the first cricket match ever to be photographed, these pictures show the game which took place on 25 July 1857 at Hunsdonbury in Hertfordshire, the seat of E. L. P. Calvert, Esq, and was played between the Royal Artillery and Hunsdonbury Cricket Club.

Roger Fenton, one of the country's leading photographers of the time (who had made his name as the semi-official photographer of the Crimean War), took at least five images of the match, using large-format wet collodion plates. Because of the low sensitivity of the process he was using, he needed the full cooperation of his subjects, who had to be carefully posed and who had to stand perfectly still for the duration of the exposure. Thus, no action shots were possible. He also needed a mobile darkroom with him, in which to coat and prepare his glass plates immediately before exposure, and then process them straight afterwards.

Writing twenty-five years later about cricket in London, Charles Dickens Jnr, a cricket fan himself, extolled the virtues of the Oval pitch, describing it as being 'as nearly perfection as can be and, in seasonable weather a wicket can be selected as true as a billiard table.' Less complimentary about Lords, he observed that it was 'notoriously a difficult ground, but the Marylebone Club has recently expended a great deal of money in draining and relaying, and a great improvement is observable.'

Above left: The teams posed for a photograph before the match. The blurred flag in the top right-hand corner of the photograph confirms that a relatively long exposure was necessary.

Left: The small crowd of spectators who gathered for the match, with the scorer on the left of the picture. This was clearly as much a social occasion as it was a sporting one, with the ladies in their finery.

Below: To get such images, Fenton would have required the total cooperation both of the teams and of the spectators, as they would have had to stand still during an exposure that may have run into several seconds. The resulting prints were mounted on specially printed boards, which listed all the players in both teams. The fact that Fenton had arranged for special mounts to be printed suggests that quite substantial numbers of prints were made, yet, surprisingly, these images remain very rare.

A golfer tees off at Chislehurst Golf Links in Kent, watched by a large group of people – perhaps the start of a competition? The golf course opened in 1894, on land surrounding the eighteenth-century Camden Place.

A ROUND OF GOLF

Given the popularity of the sport, golf is featured in remarkably few Victorian and Edwardian photographs. It more than makes up for that shortfall, however, in the number of great quotes it has drawn from the writers of the period. Amongst the literary giants who offered an opinion on the game was William Wordsworth, who offered the thought that 'golf is a day spent in a round of strenuous idleness', while Mark Twain famously observed that 'golf is a good walk spoiled.' Never one to settle for one memorable quote where several were possible, he also suggested, 'it is good etiquette not to pick up lost golf balls while they are still rolling!'

Golf can trace its origins back to the fifteenth century, when it is recorded that so many people were playing the sport, rather than practising their archery, that laws had to be passed controlling this abuse of free time. 'Futeball and golf', the decree stated, should be 'utterly cryit doun, and nocht usit!' Over five centuries later, golf is probably one of the most-played sports in the world, despite the misgivings of Wordsworth, Twain and others, while 'futeball' is of course the most watched!

It is, perhaps, a surprising fact that at the beginning of the nineteenth century, there were actually only a couple of established golf clubs in England, and perhaps no more than twenty or thirty nationwide. The oldest English club, Royal Blackheath, can be positively dated back to about 1787, although tradition places its establishment over a century earlier. It was the seventh club to be founded in Britain, the other six all being north of the border, in St Andrews, Edinburgh, Aberdeen and Musselburgh.

The mid-nineteenth century, however, saw a huge expansion in the number of golf courses (especially inland courses) in almost every part of Britain, reflecting a hugely increased enthusiasm for playing the game. England got its first seaside links course – in Devon – in 1864, and a course was opened in Wimbledon a year later.

The Royal Liverpool Golf Club at Hoylake became the first in the northwest of England when it opened in 1869. That club is also credited with starting the first amateur golf tournament in England in 1885, and the first international tournament in 1902.

Professional golfers were established as early as the 1850s, onetime close friends 'Old Tom' Morris and Allan Robertson being the most famous of the early professionals, but their working relationship had ended in the late 1840s when the 'gutty' or 'guttie' ball favoured by Morris replaced the feather-filled ball manufactured by Robertson. The early years of the twentieth century really mark the beginning of the modern game: 1902 saw the gutty golf ball facing competition, and over the following years it was replaced in Britain by rubber-cored balls, initially imported from America. Home-produced balls followed some years later.

In parallel with the growing popularity of the sport, sales of golfing postcards grew exponentially, with a surprisingly large number of different cards produced during the Edwardian years. Series of cards explained the rules; others illustrated the major events and the Open championship, while every famous golfer of the day was the subject of at least one card. Despite being produced in colour and in large numbers, such cards are relatively scarce today, and are highly prized by collectors.

Golfers on the links at Carnoustie on the east coast of Scotland. Golf has been played on Carnoustie's links since at least the middle of the sixteenth century, and probably earlier, but the golf course was only formally laid out in the 1850s, and extended to eighteen holes in the 1870s by 'Old Tom' Morris. This view dates from c.1905.

A golf match in progress on Skegness Golf Links in 1910, in conditions that are a far cry from the manicured courses we enjoy today. Links golf had been played on courses like this for hundreds of years. Today the town has several fine courses, including the North Shore Golf Club designed by the legendary James Braid, the Fife-born golfer who won the Open no fewer than five times during the Edwardian era.

A golfer makes a spectacular exit from a bunker on an unidentified golf course on this 1909 postcard.

A group of ladies practise on the putting green in front of the clubhouse at Crieff Golf Club in Scotland, c.1910. The course, by the Perth road on the outskirts of Crieff in an area of the town originally known as Dornoch, was opened in 1891. The original name is kept alive in a challenging nine-hole course at the club – the Dornock – while the main eighteen-hole course is now known as the Ferntower.

The final putt – completing a round on Lamlash Golf Course on the Isle of Arran, c.1905.

Above: This typical local amateur football team photograph is identified only as 'St Peter's FC, 1906–07', and there are no clues as to location.

Top and above opposite: Two Edwardian postcards of professional football league teams in action, playing in front of massive crowds at unknown stadiums. The date is believed to be 1907 or 1908.

FOOTBALL

Nobody can even guess at how many people in Victorian and Edwardian Britain played amateur football, and of course very few records exist to confirm the weekly attendance at Edwardian league games. However, we do know that both figures were huge. In the early days of the twentieth century, when grounds were flanked by simple open terraces (long before multi-tier grandstands, and decades before people had to get used to sitting down to watch the game), huge attendances in some of the larger stadiums were not uncommon. Newcastle United, for example, recorded a crowd of 56,000 in December 1908, only for the fans to see their heroes beaten 9–1 by local rivals Sunderland!

Football in one form or another has existed in Britain for centuries, but it was only in 1863 that the idea of a common set of rules was suggested. A group of representatives from a number of London teams met at the Freemason's Tavern in Lincoln's Inn Fields in London on 26 October 1863 and, as a result of discussions arising from a suggestion by the splendidly named Ebenezer Cobb Morley, the Football Association was inaugurated. Only one club from before that date – Notts County, founded in 1862 – is still in existence today. England's first football club – and probably the world's first as well – was Sheffield Football Club, established a few years earlier in 1855. Less than twenty years on, the FA had Scottish clubs, and even an Australian one, as members.

Three years after the professional game was introduced, the Football League was formed (by a Scotsman) in 1888, at a meeting in Anderton's Hotel in Fleet Street, London. Interestingly, it was at the same hotel thirteen years later that the Professional Photographers Association – several of whose early members took many of the photographs in this book – was formed. In that same year, Tottenham Hotspur, then of the Southern League, became the first club from outside the League to win the FA Cup!

There were twelve professional clubs in the first Football League: Accrington,

Aston Villa, Blackburn Rovers, Bolton Wanderers, Burnley, Derby County, Everton, Notts County, Preston North End, Stoke, West Brom, and Wolves. Amazingly, ten are still playing, although six of them are now in the Premiership. Preston were the League's first champions – and the second – but in the century's closing years Sunderland (who replaced Stoke) and Aston Villa were the most frequent winners. The Scottish Football League was formed in 1893, with Hibernian the first winners. While the game became increasingly professional, amateur football went through a crisis. Corinthians, believed to have been the most successful of the early amateur teams, refused to play in competitions for which a cup was awarded. Winning at all costs was not part of their ethos – they believed that the achievement of taking part and giving their best was enough to satisfy any gentleman player. They also believed that, as no gentleman would ever intentionally commit a foul, the introduction of the penalty kick was a retrograde step. They refused to take penalties when awarded, and their goalkeepers refused to save them! This sort of intransigence rapidly brought about a separation between the amateur and professional games.

Attendance at the professional game rose exponentially in the early years of the twentieth century, and as numbers rose to well over a million supporters each week, those two hours spent at the local stadium defined a Saturday afternoon.

'A Throw-in from the Touch Line' comes from the same series of football postcards as those on the previous pages. Printed in Germany, this card was number 44 in the series! The card was posted in Taunton in February 1910 to a Miss Board in Bridgwater, Somerset.

'Boy Scouts around the Camp Fire' was photographed in 1908. This postcard was sent, without any message, to a young lady card collector in Southampton in November 1909.

SCOUTING

In the closing years of the Edwardian era, being a boy scout was a novelty. The scout movement grew out of a first boys' camp organised by Lord Robert Baden-Powell on Brownsea Island off the Dorset coast in 1907. In the following year – at about the time the photograph above was taken – Baden-Powell published *Scouting For Boys*, six fortnightly publications at 4d each, which collectively became the scouting's first manual. It was this publication that formally launched the Boy Scout movement.

Initially, interest in scouting was passed amongst boys by word of mouth, with independent scout troops being formed throughout the country, giving boys a focus for team activities, sports and the pursuit of knowledge. It was, said Baden-Powell, to be a movement devoted to the development of the ideals of good citizenship.

By 1910, the movement had grown enormously, and as the reign of King Edward VII came to an end, there were believed to be something approaching 150,000 boy scouts – 125,000 of them in troops throughout the British Empire.

Many postcards were produced of local scout troops – for sale to families and friends – but few were produced by the mainstream postcard publishers for general sale.

Not to be left out, the Girl Guide movement was started in 1910 after several groups of girls got together to emulate their brothers. Baden-Powell's sister joined him in formalising the Girl Guides that same year.

Top: Catlin's Royal Pierrots perform by the walls of Aberystwyth Castle in 1906. Catlin's troupe was one of the more famous of the touring pierrot groups who performed in the Edwardian era. Will Catlin, an early impressario, had several pierrot groups touring each summer, usually putting on four shows a day on beaches, on makeshift stages, and occasionally in more traditional theatres and music halls. They were well known on both the Yorkshire coast and the North Wales coast and members of each troupe regularly met excursion trains as they arrived at the local railway station to promote their shows by passing out flyers to the arriving holidaymakers.

Above: A minstrel group performing on Mablethorpe's beach in 1904. Six performers and a pianist have attracted a considerable crowd on an otherwise very quiet beach.

Left: An amateur pierrot group performing in a Lancashire village hall, photographed c.1906.

The word 'pierrot' can be traced back to eighteenth-century France – being used to describe a pantomime character – and was taken over by the French from the seventeenth-century Italian theatre. Later, however, it was used to identify itinerant minstrels with whitened faces and baggy white costumes who went from town to town giving impromptu performances. Later still, it described the travelling concert parties and minstrel groups who put on concerts on beaches and in village halls. Pierrot and Minstrel groups could be found in just about every seaside town, with the same groups returning to the same resorts year after year and building up a loyal following from returning holidaymakers. For those who could not afford to get away from the towns and cities, local parks and town squares were turned into makeshift open-air theatres when the travelling minstrels and pierrots were in town.

Top: Large crowds regularly gathered in Llandudno's Happy Valley for performances by visiting pierrot and minstrel groups. This postcard dates from c.1907, ten years after the park opened.

Above: A professional minstrel group, with the politically incorrect name of 'Harry Frewin's White Coons', perform for an afternoon audience in a makeshift theatre near Clacton Jetty in the summer of 1910. Popular open-air entertainment like this cost much less than the summer shows staged in the nearby pavilions and music halls, and were sometimes free for those standing at the back.

43

Above: Perkins' bathing machines dominate this 1907 view of Margate beach. In the foreground donkeys await riders, and an itinerant photographer awaits customers.

Below: Scarborough beach at the height of an Edwardian summer season, complete with bathing huts, pierrots performing on a makeshift stage, and sunbathers galore. The writer of this 1909 card (postmarked 8.45pm, 26 July) starts, 'Thank you for your letter of this afternoon'; presumably the recipient read this reply over breakfast the next day.

Above opposite: Children playing in the sea at Mablethorpe, Lincolnshire, in the summer of 1903.

ON THE BEACH

'So many children', wrote Charles Dickens about his beloved Broadstairs, 'are brought down to our watering place that, when they are not out of doors, as they usually are in fine weather, it is wonderful where they are put; the whole village seeming much too small to hold them under cover. In the afternoons, you see no end of salt and sandy little boots drying on upper windowsills. At bathing time in the morning, the little bay re-echoes with every shrill variety of shriek and splash after which, if the weather be at all fresh, the sands teem with small blue mottled legs. The sands are the children's greatest resort. They cluster there, like ants: so busy burying their particular friends, and making castles with infinite labour which the next tide overthrows, that it is curious to consider how their play, to the music of the sea, foreshadows the reality of their after lives.'

The seaside holiday enjoyed immense popularity throughout the Victorian and Edwardian eras, with many towns owing their very existence to the popularity of their beaches; Clacton in Essex and New Brighton in Merseyside are notable examples.

With the expansion of the railway network and the development of coastal steamer routes, visits to the seaside were within the reach of most. Some might be able to afford only a day trip, while others managed a week, but the pleasures and health benefits of the seaside were a powerful magnet.

It is ironic that the view of the seemingly endless wide expanse of sea – one of the things we so enjoy today about the seaside – was usually all but obscured by the line of bathing machines which were then as much a part of the seaside as the sand and water themselves.

Cheap flights and guaranteed sunshine abroad have, for more than forty years, been in direct competition with indifferent weather and high prices at home, sending the British seaside holiday into serious decline.

Left: Probably considered slightly saucy in its day, this 1910 postcard of two girls in typical bathing costumes was entitled 'Skylarking at Ramsgate'.

Above: The formality of Edwardian beachwear seems at odds with the idea of a relaxing summer holiday. These women on the beach at Clacton-on-Sea are ignoring the photographer, while the little boys behind them are clearly fascinated.

Below: Every Edwardian seaside resort had at least one coloured postcard of the ubiquitous donkeys – this one is from Southport, although business does not seem to be very good on this particular day in 1908.

Right: The popularity of sea bathing at the beginning of the twentieth century is clear from the number of bathing machines that lined the shores of Britain's seaside resorts. At high tide in this 1909 view of Llandudno beach in North Wales, the bathing machines vied for space on the narrow strip of sand with a large number of deck chairs.

Opposite: The seaside pier was not as popular in Scotland as it was south of the border, but a notable exception was the resort of Portobello near Edinburgh. Well served by railways, the resort was the destination of choice for a large proportion of Edinburgh's Edwardian workforce, and offered all the expected visitor attractions. Portobello Pier, seen here in 1904, had an unenviable association with one of the more tragic events in Scotland's Victorian history – opened in 1871, it was designed by Thomas Bouch, the same engineer who built the ill-fated first Tay Bridge which collapsed into the river during a storm in 1879. The pier, however, survived until it was demolished in 1917.

Above: A large crowd gathered on the cliffs to watch the annual swimming matches at Plymouth in 1903. Few people at the time – especially women – were willing to be photographed close-up in their swimming attire!

Opposite: A crowded scene on Portobello beach in 1905, with the town's public swimming baths behind. Every Edwardian summer saw huge crowds squeeze onto the narrow beach. There were a considerable number of postcards of Portobello in Edwardian times, mainly focusing on the beach and pier, and all of them confirming the resort's position as the most popular seaside town on Scotland's east coast.

Opposite: Entitled 'A Typical Beach Scene', this postcard was published by E. J. Middleton, Stationer, Great Yarmouth, c.1905.

Opposite below: 'Sally', who sent this card to her friend Miss Jacques in July 1906, had clearly been to Burnham-on-Sea in Somerset before and had been photographed while there. 'I am sitting under the pier writing this', she wrote. 'Do you recognise me sitting on one of the donkeys?'

Below: A row of tea, food and fruit stalls, only a few feet from the sea, lines the water's edge in this busy 1905 postcard view of Southsea's Clarence Beach.

Morecambe beach on a busy day in 1905. To the left is the partly-built Morecambe Tower; it was planned as a rival to Blackpool's, but the builders ran out of money before it was completed!

TENNIS

A tennis match on the courts at Buile Hill Park, Pendleton, Salford, in the summer of 1906. This card was sent in January 1907 to a Miss Alice Taylor with the message, 'This is the place where your humble servant spent most of his evenings last summer. The scene is somewhat out of place this weather, n'est pas? [sic!]'

Perhaps it was a combination of the slowness of photography and the speed of the game, but Victorian and Edwardian images of tennis players in action are much less common than might be expected.

Victoria had been on the throne almost four decades before the game with which we are familiar was established. The 'modern' game is little more than a century and a quarter old. While 'real tennis' had been played since at least the sixteenth century, lawn tennis as we know it today dates only from about 1865. The world's first tennis club was formed in Leamington Spa in the early 1870s, and the first competition match to be played at Wimbledon took place in 1877 (W. Spencer Gore won the tournament in front of two hundred people) when the great grass court championships which remain a highlight of the tennis calendar to this day were established. At that time, only men were permitted to play, but a few years afterwards women members were admitted. By the late 1880s Wimbledon's annual tournament was known as the 'World Championship of Tennis'. Charles Dickens Jnr, in the 1888 edition of his *Dictionary of London,* noted that membership of the All England Lawn Tennis Club – men or women – was by ballot in committee, 'one black ball in five excluding', and annual subscription for playing members was two guineas. Had access to courts remained at those prices, the game would still be the exclusive domain of the well heeled!

43. NEW KENT RᵒS.E. H. Bown & 14 WISTERIA Rᵈ
31 & 33. JAMAICA Rᵈ S.E. LEWISHAM. S.E.

A carte-de-visite portrait of a young girl with her tennis racquet by Henry Bown. At first glance, the tennis racquet appears to be in rather poor condition, with some strings apparently loose, but closer inspection reveals that it is in fact tied to the metal balustrade, presumably as an aid to keeping it absolutely still during the exposure.

At the time this portrait was made, being photographed with artefacts relating to one's hobbies and pastimes was growing in popularity, and as tennis was becoming increasingly popular amongst middle-class girls, the tennis racquet may even have come from the studio's props cupboard! Henry Brown had studios on Jamaica Road, New Kent Road and 14 Wisteria Road, Eastdown Park, Lewisham. As he lists his address as both 31 and 33 Jamaica Road, this card can be dated between 1895, when he took over No. 31, and 1900.

Playing tennis at Finsbury Park, London, 1906. Finsbury Park (originally planned to be known as Albert Park after the Prince Consort) opened in 1869, and quickly established itself as a popular venue for a wide range of sports and leisure pastimes.

BOWLS

A bowls match in progress at Dewsbury Park bowling green in Yorkshire, c. 1905. Whilst most bowlers throughout Britain played on flat greens, many clubs in the Midlands and the North of England – especially Lancashire and Yorkshire – preferred the more unpredictable and challenging 'crown green'. In crown green bowling, players can send the jack across the green diagonally – indeed they can place it anywhere they wish. Both flat green and crown green bowling thrive to this day. The matches seen here are being played on a crown green.

In the seaside resort of Lamlash on the Isle of Arran, two men are engrossed in their lawn bowls match (c. 1903) against a fascinating backdrop: a Clyde steamer is tied up at the pier, while several of the Royal Navy's battleships lie at anchor offshore.

According to eminent historians, bowls is one of the oldest of outdoor games. In one form or another, it has been traced back seven millennia, and the 'modern' game can be traced back to the thirteenth century, with biased bowls being introduced three centuries later.

Amazingly, in England at least, bowls was one of the few games that the churches thought it all right to play on a Sunday in the sixteenth century. King James I, while condemning 'futeball' and 'golfe' (qv) as Sunday pastimes, approved of bowls. Scottish Presbyterians were not so generous, however, and saw it as a breach of the Sabbath!

Bowling clubs started to be introduced in the early years of Victoria's reign, but bowling greens were relatively few and far between. However, by the end of the nineteenth century it is estimated that more people played bowls than football.

As a club game, bowls was only really formalised nationally in the closing decade of the nineteenth century – a Scottish association was formed in 1892, to be followed three years later by a Midland Counties association. An English national bowls association was not formed until 1902, but throughout the Edwardian era, the number of clubs grew considerably.

While the traditional 'lawn bowls' game was getting itself organised, the rival 'crown-green' version was also in the ascendancy – albeit limited to the Midlands and the North of England – and inter-county matches were first established in the 1890s. Those first competitions were between a Yorkshire team, and a team drawn from crown-green clubs in Lancashire and Cheshire. From early on in the crown green game, professional matches, and heavy betting on the results, were commonplace.

A lawn bowls match in progress on the Bowling Green at Leith near Edinburgh, c. 1906. Bowling clubs with their own dedicated greens are recorded in Scotland in the eighteenth century in Glasgow, Edinburgh, Haddington, and Peebles. Scotland was much quicker than England at organising the sport.

WINTER SPORTS

There were, records tell us, many more bitingly cold winters in Britain in Victorian and Edwardian times than today – or at least the winter weather was more widespread and longer lasting, and our recent predecessors seem to have been more willing to get outside and enjoy it. In the days before central heating the British were made of hardier stock!

Traditional winter pastimes such as sledging, skating and curling were popular, but Britain never had enough snow to guarantee good skiing – except in remote areas of Scotland. For skiing holidays, the affluent Victorians and Edwardians travelled to France, Italy and Switzerland, where the snow was guaranteed to be plentiful.

Skating clubs, however, existed in London ('for the practice of figure skating', noted Charles Dickens Jnr in 1888) as early as 1830, in Archer's Hall, Regents Park and at No 1 Devonport Street, Hyde Park, with annual membership subscriptions of two guineas for men and one guinea for ladies.

The postcard market reflected that love of winter. Postcard views of streets and parks under heavy snow were offered for sale in many towns during winter – a further underlining of the importance of the Edwardian postcard market.

Right: On a winter holiday in France in 1905, children enjoy the pleasures of sledging.

Opposite page, top left: On holiday in 1880, this gentleman hardly seems dressed for sledging, nor does he seem particularly happy about the prospect!

Opposite page, top right: Is this what a well-dressed child might have worn when venturing outdoors in the winter of 1865? This carte-de-visite has been printed as a New Year greetings card, by scratching the lettering on to the glass plate negative, and by painting the snowflakes on to the glass with black or red ink. The winter background is a painted studio background.

Opposite: Learning to ski in 1910, from a Valentine & Company tinted postcard printed in Britain but posted from an address in Canada.

In the winter of 1908–9, Derwentwater became the biggest skating rink in the Lake District. Although this severe freeze was not especially unusual, an enterprising local photographer published postcards of the scene and offered them for sale within days! Local newspapers in the closing decades of the nineteenth century and throughout the Edwardian era regularly recorded the lake freezing over and skaters taking to the ice in huge numbers. Images like these, from only a century ago, are a powerful reminder of climate change. Canon Harwicke Rawnsley, a Lakeland clergyman, pioneer conservationist and prolific poet wrote a poem in celebration of the winter entertainment on the frozen lake. His 'Skating on Derwentwater' was published in 1908. Rawnsley was a vociferous opponent of the railways intruding into his beloved Lake District, and was a co-founder of the National Trust in 1895 along with Sir Robert Hunter and Octavia Hill.

HUNTING

How times change! While today the anti-hunting lobby has brought about a ban on hunting with hounds, and swayed public opinion strongly against the activity, a century ago hunting with hounds was an established part of British life, and a widely accepted subject for the picture postcard; there are dozens of Edwardian cards on the theme, many of them tinted, suggesting large print runs.

Fox hunting with dogs probably dates from the middle of the sixteenth century, but it reached the peak of its popularity in the nineteenth century. By the end of the eighteenth century, the red hunting tunic had become the popular dress style for the bigger and more organised hunts. It became known as 'hunting pink', according to tradition, after a London tailor named Pink, who made a hunting jacket out of the same red material that had been used for military uniforms. The hunting tradition is perpetuated in the title of 'whips' given to those responsible for organising parliamentary voting – traditionally named after the whippers-in who ensured that the hounds worked as a pack.

Opposite: An unidentified hunt photographed c.1904, and sent to a young collector in Margate. 'Another card for your book, sweetheart', wrote Dickie, from Kilburn, to Master Edward Dunne in May 1905.

Below: 'The Meet', posted from Lauder in the Scottish Borders in December 1905.

Opposite: T. Page of Rosedale Abbey photographed and published this postcard of a meet of the Farndale, Rosedale and Goathland Hunt at Rosedale. The card was posted in April 1907 to a card collector in Sheffield, the sender noting that he had 'bought this card in Goathland yesterday, but now I think it is a duplicate of one I sent some time ago.'

SHOOTING

Shooting, traditionally the hobby of the landed gentry and their friends, was a pastime enjoyed by many, and which employed thousands of people on the land: rearing and tending the birds and the deer; training and looking after the gun-dogs; maintaining the shooting grounds and grouse moors; and servicing the hunters during their sport. Gamekeepers, ghillies and beaters all owed their livelihood to this rich-man's entertainment.

The popularity of grouse shooting and deer stalking in Victorian Britain owed much to the royal family. The Prince Consort, Prince Albert, was an enthusiastic pursuer of both species, and the Balmoral estate was, at least partly, purchased and developed in order to permit him to indulge his pleasures.

While the Queen was engaged in drawing and painting the beauties of their highland landscape, Albert was out stalking across it with his guns. The Queen had once written in her diary that she found Balmoral 'so calm and solitary', and that 'all seemed to breathe freedom and peace.' Perhaps that was before Albert and his friends took up hunting!

Sir Edwin Landseer, probably best known for his canvas *Monarch of the Glen*, painted the Prince and his son (the Prince of Wales and future King Edward VII) presenting a dead stag to the Queen, so it is possible that she too enjoyed the experience.

Landseer himself was attracted by the pastime, and painted *Monarch of the Glen* during a visit in 1851 to Ardverikie (where the television series of the same name was filmed), one of the many hunting estates in Scotland. Several of his hunting pictures dominated the walls of the great house, and were all lost a few years later when the building was destroyed by fire.

This was the 'sport of kings', and King Edward VII, a keen and regular visitor to the grouse moors, went to many great estates to enjoy his sport. That it was considered the sport of kings perhaps explains why so many beautiful postcards celebrating grouse- and deer-stalking were produced during King Edward's reign.

Raphael Tuck produced many cards of grouse shooting and deer hunting, 'chromotyped in Saxony', where it was believed the finest colour printing could be purchased. By the advent of the Great War, buying cards printed in Germany was considered increasingly unpatriotic, which had the effect of driving up the quality of British colour printing. Cards like these were available nationwide, and bought by people who may never have seen or experienced the so-called 'field sports'. These examples were posted in St Ives, Chelmsford and Kirbymoorside.

Left: Grouse shooting on the Scottish moors, 1903, from Raphael Tuck's British Sports series.

Below: A hunter with his spoils, c.1910, location unknown.

Bottom: 'Deer Stalking, Returning with the Spoils', also from Tuck's British Sports series, 1903.

Above: Entitled 'Disciples of Izaak Walton', this 1908 postcard was a free giveaway to promote Shurey's Publications, a range of low-cost novels and reference books.

Below: From Tuck's famous series of British Sports, his beautiful postcard of salmon fishers landing a 20-pounder was posted in Guernsey to another Guernsey address in April 1904.

Opposite above: This stereoscopic view, entitled 'Pike Fishing, Loch of Park' has a special place in the history of photography, as it was one of the first 'instantaneous' photographs ever taken. Taken by Aberdeen photographer George Washington Wilson in 1859, the combination of shooting into the sun with a small camera and a large lens allowed Wilson to take the picture in a fraction of a second, and capture the ripples on the water. He took the lens cap off the camera with one hand, and covered the lens with his bonnet with the other – all in one-sixth of a second. When first exhibited and published, photographs like this caused widespread astonishment.

FISHING

Probably the most famous book ever written on the subject of fishing – and one which enjoyed prodigious success in the period covered by this book – was actually written in the mid- seventeenth century. The *Compleat Angler* first appeared in print in 1653, and although it went to five editions during the lifetime of its author Izaak Walton, it had fallen into almost total obscurity before it was republished at the end of the eighteenth century. In the two hundred years since then, it has appeared in literally hundreds of editions.

The Victorians and Edwardians took to fishing in a big way, and the humorous observations and endeavours of Walton's 'Piscator' obviously had the ability to make them smile – as indeed the book still does today. An edition published by Andrew Lang in 1896 contained his own essay on Walton's life and work, and in that essay, against a contemporary background of debate and vitriol about the purity of the sport, Lang clearly identifies himself as a fly-fisher, patronisingly conceding that some coarse fishermen may be good men: 'A bait-fisher may be a good man as Izaak was, but it is easier for a camel to pass through the eye of a needle. As coarse fish are usually caught only with bait, I shall not follow Izaak on to this unholy and unfamiliar ground, wherein, none the less, grow flowers of Walton's fancy, and the songs of the old poets are heard... For my part, had I a river, I would gladly let all honest anglers that use the fly cast line in it, but, where there is no protection, then nets, poison, dynamite, slaughter of fingerlings, and unholy baits devastate the fish, so that "Free Fishing" spells no fishing at all. This presses most hardly on the artisan who fishes fair, a member of a large class with whose pastime only a churl would wish to interfere.' The coarse fisherman must have appreciated Lang's inference that his hobby was really little better than poisoning or dynamiting the fish!

Even the long exposures necessary with early photography posed no problem when photographing fishermen. The popularity of the sport in Edwardian times is underlined by the number of postcards available.

A small crowd starts to gather around the bandstand in Glasgow's Queen's Park. Such free open-air concerts were a very popular Sunday afternoon entertainment. Many large factories had their own brass bands, and for them, the Sunday concert was what they practised for.

The band of a Scottish regiment (the bandmaster is dressed in a kilt) entertains visitors at the highly ornate New Bandstand at Southend-on-Sea in 1908 or 1909. Seaside bandstands invariably occupied prominent positions on the seafront.

In this 1906 postcard, a small orchestra is playing in the octagonal bandstand, which stood just in front of the entrance to the pavilion on the Grand Pier at Weston-super-Mare. The pier had been opened only three years earlier – one of very few seaside piers completed in the twentieth century. From the notices around the bandstand, we learn that it cost 2d to hire a chair, and 4d for a deck chair. Like most open-air performances in bandstands and makeshift stages, there was no charge if you stood at the back. Leaning up against the bandstand are the window sections, which sealed it off against the weather when not in use.

LISTENING TO THE BAND

There is something distinctly Edwardian in the image of a band playing to large informal crowds beneath a clear blue summer sky – the ladies in long flowing dresses and wide brimmed hats, the men looking anything but casual in closely fitting suits.

In towns up and down the country, this was a typical weekend scene – free entertainment to occupy a few hours of leisure time away from the grind of daily work. The architecture of the bandstands in civic parks ranged from the simple to exquisitely ornate constructions in cast iron.

While several excellent military bands took their turns on the bandstand, the majority of the Sunday afternoon performances were put on by voluntary amateur musicians, whose pride in their music had led them to join works bands up and down the country.

With many large factories having their own brass or silver bands, and with musicians from cotton mills, factories, railway works and collieries competing against each other in local, regional and national competitions, the quality of the music offered at these free concerts was usually of a very high order indeed. Many of the great names in bands lived on long after the employer in whose name they had been created ceased to operate, and many of them still survive and perform today.

PLEASURE BEACHES

There were already a number of well-established funfairs and pleasure beaches in America when the first ride on what would become Britain's first pleasure beach opened in Blackpool in 1896. The idea of a pleasure beach in Blackpool, where adults could become children again, originated with Alderman George Bean, and he already had a vision for the complex when the first attraction was built. That first ride was the huge Ferris wheel, which, along with the famous tower, dominated the town's skyline for many years. Blackpool Tower was only two years old when the big wheel opened, and the town's sights were set firmly on becoming Britain's number one holiday destination. By the time the two pictures opposite were taken, the town's varied attractions were already becoming extremely popular.

Ferris wheels, water chutes, flying machines, helter skelters, roller coasters, and a host of other rides became synonymous with the Edwardian seaside holiday, appearing in resorts up and down the coasts. Some of them looked none too safe – the wooden roller coaster at Folkestone being a particularly rickety looking construction.

Blackpool Pleasure Beach still occupies the same site, and the complex has consistently been voted the most popular tourist attraction in Britain. It now has 145 rides including no fewer than five roller-coasters, and attracts over seven million visitors each year!

Left: The water chute and Maxim's Flying Machine at Southport, Lancashire. Both rides opened in time for the 1905 summer season. Sir Hiram Maxim, perhaps best known for his invention of the Maxim machine-gun, was obsessed with the idea of powered flight, and his 'Captive Flying Machines' grew out of that interest, and were part of his scheme to raise money to fund his attempts at real flight! Once up to speed, these rides carried passengers in elegantly streamlined gondolas at up to 40mph, a considerable speed in those days.

Left: A group of holidaymakers watch the antics of people on the water chutes at Blackpool, c. 1909–10.

Bottom: The water chute at Weston-super-Mare was adjacent to the Birnbeck Pier, seen behind it. This postcard was produced to celebrate the chute's opening in 1905.

Opposite: Blackpool's Flying Machine, seen here in 1910, still stands more than a century after it was originally opened, and still carries passengers. With its thin wire supports, the gondolas feel like they are really flying. In 1904 when it was opened, in the days long before passenger flight was a reality, it is hardly surprising these machines were so popular! Today the gondolas carry advertising for Ryanair. In addition to the Southport and Blackpool rides, 'Flying Machines' were popular attractions at Earls Court and Crystal Palace in London, and in Philadelphia, Coney Island and elsewhere in America. By fitting one of the Crystal Palace gondolas with wing flaps and controls, Maxim learned much about flight aerodynamics. The Blackpool ride is the only one still operational.

69

Nottingham Goose Fair, c.1908. Looking at this splendid view of the fairground rides, which had become a central feature of the fair, it is difficult to believe that merry-go-rounds were actually banned by the City Council in the 1820s. They returned in 1855 with a manually cranked carousel, but by the end of the century, the square was packed with steam-powered rides on an ever-grander scale. The Goose Fair has been held in Nottingham for five hundred years – it was first mentioned in 1541 – and until the 1920s it was held in the city centre. A new site for the event, about a mile from the old, was opened in 1929.

A busy scene during the annual Wakes Week Fair in Tommyfields, Oldham, Lancashire, 1905.

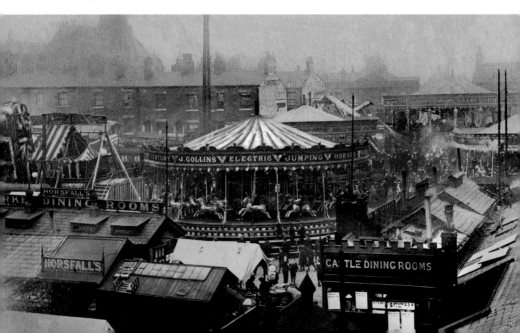

ALL THE FUN OF THE FAIR

For those who could afford it, the pleasures of a week – or even just a couple of days – at the seaside were irresistible. But what of those who could not afford to go away? For them, the entertainment came to town – in the form of huge fairs with brightly painted merry-go-rounds and other rides. Many of these fairs were originally associated with religious festivals, but in the industrialised towns in the nineteenth century, the 'Wakes Fair' was specifically timed to entertain the workforce during the week or fortnight during which the mills and factories were closed. In Oldham, Wigan, Manchester and elsewhere, the Wakes probably had religious origins somewhere in the mists of time, but as far as the miners and cotton workers were concerned, this was a few days' respite from the rigours of work – a brief period when they could let their hair down.

The tradition of the Wakes Week Fair dates from the 1870s when workers started to be given (unpaid) holidays. In many towns, fairs associated with the religious calendar were moved to whichever week in the summer the mill and factory owners had selected for their annual closure. In many northern towns, the Wakes Week tradition survived well into the 1970s, with workers still electing to take their holidays during the same two weeks each year. The annual summer fairs still visit these towns during the week or weeks that were formerly identified with the annual Wakes holiday period.

St Giles' Fair, Oxford, from a photograph by Henry Taunt & Co, used on a 1905 postcard. The fair was originally associated with St Giles' church, and was established in the seventeenth century. By the early nineteenth century it had become a general fair, and evolved over the century into a massive annual event with fairground rides jammed together along the streets. On 24 September 1889, *The Oxford Chronicle* noted that 'the roundabouts were numerous, and included the old-fashioned ones turned with a handle to the latest improvements in steam-powered engines', and that 'Day's menagerie, containing a collection of five hundred animals, including lions, tigers, leopards, bears, hyenas, packs of wild wolves, ostriches, pelicans, vultures, owls, &c., was filled from morning to night.' Bible stalls, however, remained a regular feature of the fair.

A picnic party at Gilsland's 'Dropping Stone' (on the border between Cumbria and Northumberland) in the 1860s was considered to be important enough for a local photographer to record the event for posterity in 3D. As the stereoscope was a popular entertainment in many a Victorian parlour and drawing room, it is more than likely that many of those attending the picnic bought copies as a memento of the day.

The author's grandfather as a young man (front middle) with his family enjoying a picnic – with best china teacups of course – in the summer of 1901 or 1902, and (opposite page) the family clearing up after another picnic that same summer.

A SUMMER PICNIC

The formality of dress and behaviour evident in photographs of Victorian and Edwardian holidaymakers is a far cry from the relaxed codes of today. The picnic was a popular pastime of Queen Victoria, but alfresco eating and drinking did not mean the abandonment of the standards and etiquette of the drawing room and dining room. Good china was transported in heavy wicker baskets, and good table manners remained the order of the day even if there was no table!

There is a sense, in reading Queen Victoria's published diaries, that 'we stopped for our tea, about twenty minutes to four, and seated ourselves on the grass', is in fact a record of something close to complete abandonment of normal behaviour as far as Her Majesty was concerned!

A TRIP ON A PLEASURE STEAMER

A trip on a pleasure steamer was one of the most popular aspects of the Victorian and Edwardian summer, and that popularity is epitomised in the competition amongst steamer owners. Competition became intense in some of the major resorts, with large owners trying every trick they could think of to squeeze single-ship owners out of business. On the south coast, the large steamer fleet operated by A.S. Campbell dominated. The pleasure steamers varied in size from tiny little vessels, which took perhaps no more than half a dozen visitors on short trips on the rivers, lakes and lochs of Britain, up to massive paddle steamers capable of carrying hundreds of passengers. These large ships often combined the role of pleasure steamer with that of working ferry.

From the world-famous 'Wigan Pier' on the Leeds–Liverpool Canal, daily cruises set off for a short excursion down the canal to the nearest lock gate and back. On the lakes and lochs, steamers – many of them owned by the big railway companies – connected with excursion trains and offered city dwellers a day out in a landscape about as far removed from their urban environment as could be imagined. On Loch Katrine in the Trossachs region of Scotland, a

Opposite top: The paddle steamer *Suffolk* sets off from Ipswich to Lowestoft and Harwich. For many, this was the best part of their day at the seaside; for others, the service connected with coastal steamers to destinations and holiday resorts much further afield.

Opposite bottom: The steamer *Koh-i-Noor* off Clacton, laden with more than enough passengers to give today's health and safety officers a nightmare!

Above: The steamer *Rob Roy* gets up steam in readiness for the first trip of the day up Loch Katrine from Trossachs Pier. Since the steamer service was introduced in the 1840s, only three vessels have operated the service – two called *Rob Roy* and the 1900-built *Sir Walter Scott*, which still serves the loch today.

Below: At Trossachs Pier in 1903, a fleet of coaches is preparing for departure after picking up passengers from *Sir Walter Scott*, the stern and funnel of which can be seen in the distance. Their tour of Scotland would almost certainly have included a sail on Loch Lomond as well.

sail on the steamer *Rob Roy* and later on the *Sir Walter Scott* was an established part of many Victorian and Edwardian tours around the places associated with Scott's life and works; Thomas Cook's very first package tour of Scotland in 1843 included that as a highlight! The *Sir Walter Scott*, launched in 1900, still plies the loch in the summer season. Pleasure steamers also still serve several of the English Lakes.

Opposite: A photograph from the days when maximum permissible numbers of passengers were apparently of no concern to the steamer operators: if you could squeeze on board, you got on board! The heavily laden PS *Royal Sovereign* sets sail from London Bridge on her way to Clacton-on-Sea in 1905.

Above: Another huge crowd aboard the PS *Wemyss Castle* as she prepares to leave the West Pier at Leith, c.1903. The 172-ton steamer had been built in Glasgow as the PS *Gareloch* in 1872, and she regularly sailed from Leith to North Berwick, and round the Fife coast.

Below: The PS *Ivanhoe* passing Barton Bridge during a season as a pleasure cruiser on the Manchester Ship Canal in 1894, shortly after the canal opened. Built in 1880 for use on the Clyde, *Ivanhoe* had a working life of almost forty years. Her stay on the Ship Canal was not a financial success, and she returned to Clyde service in 1895. She was broken up in 1920.

A group of ladies and a small girl are captured by a postcard photographer while promenading on Clacton Pier in 1909. Did they return to the resort in 1910 and buy copies of 'their' postcard to take home and send to their friends?

PROMENADING

Promenading as a social custom has its roots in the boulevards of Paris, and later in the fine streets and parks of London, where the beneficial effects of 'taking the air' could be combined with a display of social status and wealth.

Seaside piers were originally little more than landing stages for steamers. But with the Victorian love of dressing up and promenading, they became, by the end of the 1860s, the places to be seen on balmy summer days. On holiday, a lady's mornings could be spent sitting on the beach, but never paddling. Only children and servants displayed themselves so informally in public. Ladies sat and watched until lunchtime. After lunch, dressed in their finery, they walked – to see and to be seen.

The use of piers and promenades for these public displays was, in large measure, responsible for the development of the pier as an entertainment complex. Bandstands were erected at the end of the pier, later to develop into the elaborate pier pavilions, and on many of the longer piers, shelters punctuated the long walk from the shore, offering protection from the wind and rain for at least a number of the promenaders.

The provision of rudimentary shelter was the least the pier-owners could do – most of them were charging the promenaders between 2d and 6d in the 1870s for the pleasure of taking their bracing walk. Southport charged 6d admission unless the person was buying a steamer ticket and, in the days before disabled rights and OAP discounts, one shilling per bath chair!

In vivid contrast with the high charges at Southport, the Wellington Pier Company in Great Yarmouth was a real bargain: admission for promenaders was set at just one penny for adults, and a halfpenny for children! No wonder it proved very popular.

Opposite: Taking a leisurely walk along Bournemouth Pier was a popular form of recreation in the early years of the twentieth century. Posted as a Christmas card in 1905, this animated view was an ideal reminder of those simple summer pleasures. It was sent to a family in Bury St Edmunds from some friends they had met on holiday.

Ladies promenading on Southport's Pier on a quiet summer's day in 1909. Southport prided itself in offering a slightly more sophisticated experience than the brashness of Blackpool.

A busy scene on the jetty at Great Yarmouth, 1910. At the time, Great Yarmouth was both one of the country's busiest herring fishing ports, and a highly popular holiday resort.

By the Edwardian era, although social expectations were more relaxed, the tradition of dressing up and taking a stroll was as popular as ever. Large wooden trunks were needed to contain the several changes of clothes people would need for different times of the day.

Left: Everyone in their finery: large crowds on the seafront taking part in the daily promenading ritual in Cliftonville, Margate, as captured in this postcard view from the summer of 1910.

Below: Elegantly dressed Edwardian holidaymakers photographed as they ended their long walk along Cleethorpes Pier, from a card posted in August 1909. 'Enjoying ourselves', wrote Alf to his friend in Manchester, 'ripping splendid weather, and plenty of girls here – a grand spot.' Originally 1,200 feet long but only 20 feet wide, the walk to the concert hall at the seaward end must have seemed interminably long; however, that hall had been demolished after a fire in 1903 and the new pavilion, seen here, had been built much closer to the shore.

An early motor car makes its way down Berrow Road in Burnham-on-Sea, Somerset, in 1905.

Actress Godwynne Earle was obviously enjoying considerable success on the Edwardian stage when she posed for the postcard photographer (c.1904) to show off her newly purchased car.

MOTORING

There were just two cars exhibited at Britain's first 'Horseless Carriage Exhibition' at Tunbridge Wells in 1895. When the first proper motor show was held at the Crystal Palace in January 1903, over two hundred different makes and models were on display. Ten thousand people attended the event – substantially more visitors than the 8,000 drivers there were on the road at the time! Interest in the motor car was immense, even if the price was beyond the reach of all but the wealthy.

Until the passing of the Motor Car Act of 1903, cars had no registration number, drivers had no licences, and the use of the roads by 'horseless carriages' was very lightly regulated. Under the 1903 Act, however, drivers were required to register their vehicles with their local authority, and to pay five shillings for a driving licence – there was no driving test, just the simple process of filling in a form and handing over the money.

Earl Russell, grandson of the former prime Minister and brother of philosopher Bertrand Russell, reportedly camped all night outside the offices of London County Council to make sure he was first in the queue when car registration numbers were issued, and thus acquired the plate 'A1'.

The 1903 Act became law on 1 January 1904, and amongst its other provisions, a whole list of driving offences was introduced. Less than two weeks later, one Henry Smith entered the history books by becoming the first person to appear in court charged with being drunk in charge of a motor car, and with failing to have a valid driving licence. Mr Smith claimed he was tired rather than drunk, and also that he didn't know he needed a licence. He was fined £10 on the first count – half the maximum penalty prescribed by the Act – and five shillings on the second count, instead of the stipulated £5. In 1904, these were huge sums of money, but as motoring was the exclusive domain of the wealthy, the fines were probably in keeping with their ability to pay!

An uncommon sign of wealth in Brunswick Terrace, Weymouth, photographed c.1909, with a single motor car parked outside one of the elegant villas that overlooked the shore.

Above: Queen Victoria's children in a tableau entitled 'The Seasons', photographed in 1854 at Buckingham Palace by Roger Fenton. Even royalty, it seems, loved dressing up for the camera.

Below: Gorleston-on-Sea Pageant, 1908, with the vicar in his role of 'The Master of Knights'.

Opposite page: Bury St Edmund's Pageant in 1907, from locally produced picture postcards.

PAGEANTS & DRESSING UP

Pageantry has been an established part of the British tradition for centuries, and was a regular subject for the artist's brush throughout Victorian times. For much of photography's first half-century, however, the camera was only very rarely turned towards the many pageants held up and down the country, as the long exposures necessary made spontaneous pictures impossible.

Until then, the constructed 'tableaux' (opposite page top left) had to suffice. But once the sensitivity of films had reached a level where 'instantaneous' pictures could be taken, the animated scenes at annual pageants were obvious subjects.

Local pageants involved people from all walks of life, and while some pageants continued to produce postcards based on artists' interpretations of the festivities, others, like Bury St Edmunds, enthusiastically embraced the new medium, giving the participants their moment of fame.

As the postcards, published annually within just a few days of the event, were printed in limited numbers for local use and had a relatively short shelf life, most were in black and white. Topicality was of the essence, and getting the cards printed quickly was an important issue if maximum sales were to be realised. Some towns, however – like Gorleston on Sea – went to the additional time and expense of having the cards printed in colour to celebrate the annual dressing-up festival.

Lyulph's Tower, Ullswater.

Visiting Lyulph's Tower, Ullswater, photographed by Thomas Ogle, c. 1865. Carte-de-visite prints like this, ready-mounted on card, were designed to fit in the family album and be kept as reminders of a holiday or a day out – the role later taken on by the picture postcard.

A FEW DAYS IN THE COUNTRY

Photography and the tourist trade grew up together. As soon as the middle classes had the time and the money to travel into the countryside, a whole market grew up to service their every need. As noted earlier, Thomas Cook's first package holiday took place in 1845 – to the Scottish Trossachs – and within a few years, guidebooks to explain the beauties of the coutryside were available to visitors. For those city-dwellers who had rarely, if ever, ventured into the countryside, some guides even explained to them how they should respond to the beauty of the landscape.

Photography became part of that education, with scenic views being produced by entrepreneurial photographers like Francis Frith and George Washington Wilson. These large studios claimed, by the 1870s, to have photographed every scenic view and tourist attraction in the country, and to have prints for sale in a variety of sizes to suit all budgets.

When the large view print gave way to the ubiquitous carte-de-visite – the small card-mounted view that could be slipped into the family album alongside portraits of family and friends – local photographic studios up and down the country got in on the act. The carte-de-visite in the 1860s, like the one above, was the picture postcard of its day – or even the guidebook, as many had descriptive texts printed on the reverse of the card. Local photographers produced literally hundreds of different views for the new generation of tourists to take home as mementos of their visit.

The postcard assumed the same role after 1900, its introduction coinciding with a rise in interest in exploring the countryside amongst the increasingly affluent middle classes.

Two coaches crowded with passengers cross Lake Windermere in this postcard (c.1906), while the two crewmen control the ferry from the back. 'This is the way we crossed the Lake', wrote an unknown sender to Miss U. L. Price in Boston, Massachusetts, adding, 'the smoke stack is for the engine. The chain which is wound up on a wheel is not shown in the picture.'

Enjoying a ride in the country, location unknown, c.1870. 1/6th plate ambrotypes like this were taken by itinerant photographers. The completed picture, in its little paper-covered wooden frame, would probably have cost sixpence, and would have been presented to the family, fully processed and framed, before they continued on their way. While the location remains a mystery, it must have been a sufficiently popular place for there to have been a photographer waiting to capture the scene.

Coaches crowded with visitors descend the 'Devil's Elbow' in the Lake District on the return journey to Keswick after a day out at Buttermere. This photograph was taken by the Abraham brothers of Keswick, probably at least a dozen years before this postcard was published in 1904. The Abraham studio, established in 1866, produced hundreds of fine views of the Lakes. The Lake District was where the British tourist industry was first established – the publication of Thomas West's 1778 *Guide to the Lakes* is often cited as the catalyst. In his book West listed 'viewing stations' where exquisite views of the landscape could be enjoyed.

The Snowdon Mountain Railway offered a more relaxing route to the summit for the less energetic visitors. The single carriage was pushed up the mountain by a small steam locomotive.

hills led to many hundreds of wonderful photographs. When they started taking pictures in the 1890s, they were using glass plates, and regularly hauled and carried 15–20kg of equipment and materials up steep slopes and vertical cliff faces – a far cry from today's photographers with their lightweight and easy-to-use digital cameras. The brothers' first mountain pictures were produced at the instigation of the climber and writer O. G. Jones, who needed illustrations for his classic book *Rock Climbing in the English Lake District,* which was published in 1897 by their father, George Abraham Snr.

Above left: Climbers on the Crazy Pinnacle, Crib Goch, Snowdon, photographed in 1907 for a postcard published as part of the Grosvenor Series and printed in Germany.

Above right: This 1905 Autochrome card was published by the Pictorial Stationery Company of London. The scene is the summit of Scafell Pike.

Climbers on the cliffs at Flamborough Head on the Yorkshire Coast in 1906. 'This spot is between Scarboro' and Bridlington – nearer to the latter' wrote an anonymous friend on a postcard sent to Miss Severmore in London in 1907. 'It stands far out into the sea. Plenty of climbing to be done in this part – nothing but hills and cliffs everywhere!'

SPORTS DAY

Sports days were a regular annual feature of the country calendar, and were as common as agricultural shows and horse shows. Nowhere in England was the annual sporting gathering more important than in Grasmere in the Lake District; the Grasmere Sports are still held to this day. Wrestling, sprinting, fell-running and other sports were all watched by huge local crowds. While most sources date the first recorded account of the sports as 1852, others give a date of 1864 or 1868. The August 2002 sports were celebrated as the 150th birthday of the event. The founder members of the Grasmere Sports included one William Baldry, a local professional photographer, who in 1868 was accorded the title of 'Official Photographer to the Sports', a role he fulfilled with great enthusiasm for over thirty years. It was shortly after Baldry's appointment that George Steadman became wrestling champion – and remained champion for several years longer than Baldry remained official photographer!

One of the highlights of the Grasmere event was the Guides' Race, and this annual event was the subject of intense competition amongst the professional guides who helped tourists trek through the hills. In addition to the prize for winning the race, prizes were also awarded for the best-dressed guides, and some of them turned up in pretty eccentric attire!

Left: The most famous of all the Cumberland wrestlers, George Steadman, dominated the sport in the late 1890s. In 1896, at the age of 51, he won the Grasmere Sports wrestling competition for the thirtieth time. This photograph was taken in 1896 by Lakeland photographer Henry Mayson.

Below: A tinted postcard from 1903 celebrating the world-famous Grasmere Sports, and one of its highlights, the wrestling tournament.

A NICE CUP OF TEA

The British have long been renowned for their love of 'a nice cup of tea' (never just a cup of tea, always a 'nice' one), so it is not surprising that in an era where the postcard celebrated just about every aspect of Edwardian life, the ritual of tea drinking featured in several splendid cards.

From beaches to exhibition sites, country parks to municipal parks, the tea shop, tea garden or tea pavilion was invariably packed on a summer's afternoon, and many sold their own postcards to their appreciative patrons.

Opposite top: This 1907 view of an outdoor tearoom on the Isle of Bute, near Kildavanan on Ettrick Bay, underlines the formality of the Edwardian dress code expected even on holiday.

Opposite: A 'night' scene in Thom's Tea Gardens in the Municipal Gardens, Southport, c.1905.

Above: The Tea Garden at the Franco-British Exhibition at the White City, London, 1908.

Below: The Tea House in Harrogate's Valley Gardens, c.1905. 'I had my tea here when I went to Harrogate', wrote Lilian to her friend Harold in August 1906.

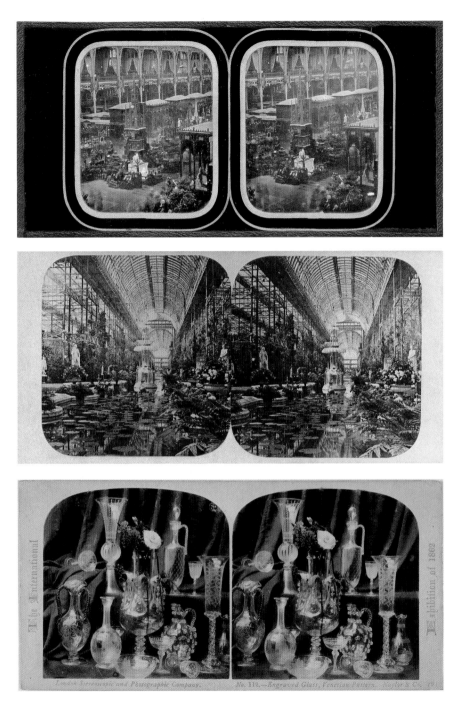

VISITING EXHIBITIONS

The popularity of visiting exhibitions can be traced back to the 1851 Great Exhibition at the Crystal Palace in Hyde Park. People visited the spectacle in their millions, and the event was copied all over the world as well as in many other locations in Britain. The 1951 Festival of Britain marked the centenary of organised exhibitions. Between 1851 and 1910, some remarkably lavish events were staged, many of which were celebrated in photographs and early postcards.

Photographic sales kiosks were set up within the Crystal Palace in Hyde Park in 1851, and at the rebuilt complex at Sydenham later in the decade. Photographers paid considerable sums for their franchises, and the practice of buying photographic mementoes of visits to these great events was quickly established. The firm of Negretti & Zambra, which had a franchise within the Crystal Palace at Sydenham, offered photographs of interior views and exhibits in a variety of formats, from small prints to be put in the family album, and stereocards for viewing in the drawing room 3D stereoscope, through to large prints to be pasted into scrap books. Unique daguerreotypes (direct positive images on silvered metal plates) and ambrotype positives on glass were sold at premium prices at events up until the mid-1850s. Thereafter, the paper print predominated. These photographs established a market that developed into the guidebooks and postcards we expect today.

Opposite top: A rare stereoscopic daguerreotype showing the interior of the 1855 Exposition Universelle in Paris. Images like these were bought as souvenirs and brought back to Britain by visitors. The ghostly figures in the foreground are the shadowy impressions of visitors who did not stand still for the duration of the lengthy exposure. Only the seated visitors have been captured fully.

Opposite middle: The interior of the Crystal Palace at Sydenham, c.1855. For affluent visitors, a set of three stereocards could be purchased for about two shillings.

Opposite bottom: A glassware exhibit from the 1862 International Exhibition. Over six million people visited the fair, which was held in Kensington between May and November 1862 on the site now occupied by the Science Museum and the Natural History Museum.

Above: The exhibition train which ferried visitors around the White City site from 1908.

Many dedicated exhibition sites were developed in the country's major cities in the early years of the twentieth century, the White City being perhaps the best known and the most regularly used; it also hosted the 1908 Olympic Games.

So popular did these events become in Edwardian times that postcard publishers Valentines of Dundee produced extensive ranges of cards to celebrate each new exhibition. Sometimes the same view was overprinted with details of whichever exhibition was currently using each site, and post offices with special postmarks were set up inside the exhibition grounds. The huge demand for these cards is affirmed by the fact that so many beautifully coloured cards were offered for sale; Valentines even had their own sales kiosk at the White City.

For the 1908 Scottish Exhibition in Edinburgh, an exhibition ground was developed. It was serviced by its own tram service, and by regular trains to the nearby Exhibition Station specially built for the event by the North British Railway Company. The organisers were rewarded by the huge crowds that attended the event.

Pulsford's Map and Guide of Edinburgh, published in 1908, reported that the exhibition site had been 'granted by the Edinburgh Corporation for the purpose' and continued, 'the site consists of about 40 acres, on the city boundary, a little over a mile west of Princes Street. The grounds are admirably adapted for the purpose, being well provided with shady trees and commanding fine views of Edinburgh and the surrounding country, with Corstorphine Hill close by on the north and the Pentlands on the south. Included in the grounds is the Old Mansion House of Saughton Hall with the beautiful gardens adjoining. The main buildings comprise the Industrial Hall, Machinery Hall, Fine Arts Gallery, Concert Hall, Canadian Pavilion, Winter Garden, etc. Besides these there are Russian and Irish pavilions, a Model Hospital, Small Holdings, Refreshment Saloons, Band and Grand Stands, Kiosks and other buildings.' The exhibition ground thus had a layout and character echoing that of several other locations throughout Britain and mainland Europe.

Above: A large-format postcard of the Japan-British Exhibition held at the White City in 1910. Dozens of different cards were offered for sale at White City and, while this one was unique to the 1910 event, many cards produced for the Franco-British Exhibition of 1908 were simply over-printed for sale during subsequent exhibitions.

Left: The 'Moulin Rouge Helter-Skelter' at the 1908 Scottish Exhibition in Edinburgh. After the exhibition closed, several of the fairground rides were rebuilt on nearby Portobello's pleasure beach.

Opposite: On this card of 'A Busy Day at the Franco-British Exhibition', Cissie wrote, 'We are off to the White City again today. Splendid weather.' The card is dated 17 October, so Cissie's visit was not to the exhibition, but to the 1908 London Olympic Games.

A large crowd lines the motor racing circuit along the seafront at Bexhill-on-Sea in 1905, while a photographer stands with his tripod-mounted camera to record the event. Bexhill enjoyed five years unchallenged as the home of British motor sport before Brooklands opened in 1907.

MOTOR RACING

Motor racing originated in France in the mid-1890s, but the first race to be held on British soil took place in the early years of the twentieth century: in May 1902 in the perhaps unlikely location of Bexhill-on-Sea.

The idea originated with Earl De La Warr, who saw interest in motor sport as being a means of raising the profile of the town, much of which he owned. The Bicycle Boulevard, which ran along part of De La Warr Parade, had the makings of an ideal sprint circuit. For his first racing event, the Earl, in collaboration with the Automobile Club of Great Britain, attracted over two hundred entries, and huge crowds came along to watch the spectacle of cars doing 50mph along the seafront – over four times the legal speed limit of the day. The event became hugely popular, and the Earl drew up plans to develop a proper racing circuit for the town, but they never came to fruition. By the summer of 1907, the focus of motor sport had moved to Brooklands near Weybridge, to the world's first purpose-built motor racing circuit. The first event at the new circuit was held on 28 June (the day the circuit was officially opened), and three Napier cars raced. The first 'official' meeting was held on 6 July 1907, again attracting large crowds, and Brooklands quickly became the centre of British motor sport. At the fourth meeting at the new circuit, in September 1907, only two months after it had opened, amateur driver Vincent Herman, driving a 52hp Minerva car, became the sport's first fatality.

PLAYING CARDS

Above: 'A Card Party', a tinted stereocard from the early 1860s. The party scene depicted in this card was posed in a studio, and the 'card players' were out-of-work actors and actresses. Teams of women and children were employed by the company to colour the images individually – usually each person applying one colour in an early production-line process.

Below: A foursome playing cards in the Billiard Room of the Clarion Cycling Club, Handforth, Cheshire, c.1905. The Clarion Club was founded originally in Birmingham in 1894 with a view to combining the dual pursuits of cycling and socialism – their name borrowed from *The Clarion*, Robert Blatchford's socialist newspaper of the day. The Handforth club was an early and highly successful venture, first opening its doors in c.1896.

Above: A traffic jam in Boulter's Lock near Maidenhead, c.1910, watched by a huge crowd on the towpath and bridge.

Below: A group of local men watch visitors in rowing boats pass through a lock at Goring (c.1907).

Opposite: Six passengers about to set sail in a small steamboat at Teddington Lock in 1906.

BOATING

The British love affair with boats is as old as boats themselves, but in the late nineteenth century, with an increase in leisure time, people took to the water in huge numbers.

Many canals, lakes, lochs and rivers sported pleasure steamers (illustrated elsewhere in this book) but also offered small craft for hire to the more adventurous. A few hours, or perhaps day out in the fresh air vigorously rowing, travelling at the leisurely pace of a few miles an hour, was a highly attractive proposition.

For the rather more affluent members of Edwardian society, the opportunity to own one's own boat, and sail it through many of the locks which made large stretches of the Thames navigable, often created traffic jams that would make today's motorways seem relatively quiet!

The image of Boulter's Lock at Maidenhead (opposite) is a typical example. Indeed, long queues and crowds of people were so much a feature of the river at Boulter's Lock that several rival postcard companies produced coloured views of the place.

Municipal parks had boats for hire on their serpentine lakes, and small skiffs could be hired by the hour on several of the English Lakes well before the end of Victoria's reign.

Even the queen herself was not averse to the occasional boat trip, as long as the weather was fine. Expeditions on steamers on the Scottish lochs figure from time to time in her diaries, including one planned sail on Loch Lomond, which she abandoned at the last minute due to heavy rain, leaving Albert to sail alone!

Years later, in 1869, with her daughters Beatrice and Louise, she sailed the length of Loch Katrine on the steamer *Rob Roy,* recalling in her diaries that ten years earlier she had sailed on

that same vessel with Prince Albert when she had opened the Glasgow Waterworks, which drew (and still draws) water from the loch. That day, with the boat safely at anchor, they had taken tea on the deck, before returning to their coaches and the journey back to Invertrossachs where they were staying.

Further diary entries in 1877 recall a short crossing in a rowing boat at Gairloch in the Highlands. 'It was delightful', wrote the queen, 'rowing through these wooded and rocky islands, with the blue, calm loch – not another sound but the oars. One might even believe the queen herself had been at the oars!'

The popularity of boating, on lakes, lochs, rivers and canals, was reflected in the popularity of postcards illustrating the pastime. Using that measure, boating was, in Edwardian times, very popular indeed!

This superb 'Photochrom' print from the late 1890s depicts a timeless scene at Bannantyne on the Kyles of Bute, with a small sailing dinghy being prepared for a sail around the bay. The Photochrome Company, originally from Zurich, produced what it claimed were 'real colour photographs' of many resorts and beauty spots in Britain. In reality they were monochrome photographs printed in up to fourteen colours to create a very colourful effect – sometimes more natural than others. This view, heavily retouched, is perhaps more like a painting than a photograph, but still offers us an evocative glipse of an enduring pastime.

A small rowing boat at the jetty at Eccleston Ferry on the River Dee near Chester, c.1910, while a small passenger steamer takes on passengers.

Women are rowing all three boats in this view of the canal at Hythe, Kent, from a card posted in 1907.

CROQUET

When this picture of the South Croquet Lawn at Beaumont Hall was taken in Clacton-on-Sea (*c.*1910), the game was enjoying something of a revival. Ultimately, however, it never again rivalled lawn tennis in popularity.

The game of croquet seems quintessentially English, and forever locked into that period at the height of Victoria's reign and in the years leading up to the Great War. Despite some claims that it is based on a thirteenth-century French game, croquet as the Victorians knew it was introduced into England only in the 1850s. By the 1860s it was immensely popular, but almost disappeared as lawn tennis swept into popularity in the 1870s. The All England Croquet Club was formed in 1868, and the new body leased land in Wimbledon in 1869. Only six years later, the club gave one of their lawns up for tennis, and by 1877 the club's name had been changed to the All England Croquet and Lawn Tennis Club.

Croquet enjoyed a significant revival in the 1890s, with the United All England Croquet Association being formed in 1896. Under British rules, the game was played on a lawn – known as a court – measuring 35 yards by 28 yards, and by teams of one or two players. In America, it was an altogether more intimate affair, being played on a court measuring a mere 10 yards by 20 yards.

Opposite: The Plantation, Exmouth, featured on many postcards during the Edwardian era. The same group of clean, tidy and well-dressed girls – walking, playing or just sitting – appears in several of the pictures, so it is likely that the photographer brought them along! The photograph probably dates from around 1906. The wooden hoop was a popular toy – found just as frequently in schools as part of the gymnastics or physical education class.

CHILDREN PLAYING

The old Victorian adage that children should be 'seen but not heard' suggests a society where children's youthful enthusiasms were suppressed; however, photographic evidence suggests this was not the case. Certainly as far as middle- and upper-class children were concerned, their parents indulged them as much as they could afford, and were happy to have them photographed with the results of those indulgences. Thus, many carte-de-visite images of children include favourite toys, dolls and other playthings.

The profusion of children's toys in early photographs, however, may reveal a clever sales gimmick on the part of the photographer. Many studios offered the opportunity for parents to be photographed in clothes they could never afford, and for children to be photographed with toys they could never own. Thus, while the horse and cart (opposite bottom right) may have belonged to the little boy in the photograph, the elegant rocking horse (opposite bottom left) more probably belonged to the studio, despite the obviously fashionable dress of the little girl!

Opposite page left and far left: Carte-de-visite photographs from around 1860 and 1875. These would have been the children of wealthy parents, judging by the quality of their clothes. The rocking horse was a common motif in child portraits.

Above: 'Children with Toys' is a Victorian thermoplastic portrait case from c.1858. Cases like these were amongst the world's first commercial products to use moulded plastic. Inside this little case, two child portraits on glass are preserved, set in a bed of deep red velvet.

Top: Entitled 'Driving His Carriage and Pair', does this 1906 postcard show the ultimate child's toy? Many fanciful postcards like this were produced during the Edwardian era. They were often used as greetings cards – this one was sent to Master George Edie on the occasion of his birthday in November 1910.

Right: Photographed by an itinerant photographer in the 1870s, this well-dressed young lady has invited her favourite dolly to join her in the photograph. Like every ambrotype photograph, this image is unique – if the girl's mother wanted more than one copy of the portrait, then several separate pictures would have had to be taken.

COURTSHIP

Romantic relationships between young men and their young ladies have been the subject of many humorous photographic tableaux since the earliest days of the Victorian carte-de-visite in the early 1860s. Subjects as serious as love and marriage, and life and death, were inevitably treated in a light-hearted manner.

Many of the series of cartes and stereocards were the photographic equivalent of the comedy sketches which could have been seen in contemporary music halls, or the cartoons found in magazines. 'Before Marriage' and 'After Marriage' (below) were typical of many studio tableaux which explored the difference between the thoughtfulness of the hopeful suitor and the callousness of the husband once the 'catch' had been secured! That tradition continued well into the picture postcard era, with many images perpetuating age-old stereotypes about the inevitable rituals of courtship and marriage.

Many series of light-hearted 3D stereocards on the subject were produced and marketed from the 1850s through to the 1880s, many of them a little risqué, and dealing with such subjects as the wily but feckless husband flirting with the maid while his wife was out of the house.

In the Edwardian era, tinted postcards were sent by friends either to the suitor or the young lady, invariably with a wry message about the likelihood of impending nuptials!

BEFORE MARRIAGE.

Copyright.

AFTER MARRIAGE.

Copyright.

ENJOYING A PINT OF BEER

'In 1879', wrote Charles Dickens Jnr in 1887, 'a company of which Lord Shaftsbury was president, made the first attempt on a large scale to give the lower section of the inhabitants of London a chance of escape from the public-house. The object of this company was to establish attractive places of refreshment in the "more densely peopled parts of London, and elsewhere, to serve as a counter-attraction to the public-house and the gin palace." It would appear from the interesting brochure by Mr. Hepple Hall, that the enterprise for some reason or another did not succeed so well as its promoters expected.' The 'some reason' to which Dickens alludes was the fanciful idea that the frequenters of alehouses would willingly forgo that pleasure for the rather more expensive delights of a well-presented cup of coffee! Perhaps Lord Salisbury's company was, simply, rather ahead of its time.

Public houses and gin palaces in the 1870s had a terrible reputation, and an attempt to restrict their opening hours with the 'Intoxicating Liquor (Licensing) Bill' of 1872 had met with huge public outcry. More than three-quarters of a million people are said to have protested against the Bill, which sought to curb completely unrestricted drinking. It was eventually passed as the 1872 Licensing Act, and enshrined in it were a number of offences that remain

to this day, and one which (happily) isn't: it included the offence of 'simple drunkenness'! It also became an offence to be drunk in charge of a horse, a cow, a carriage or a steam engine, and to be drunk in charge of a loaded firearm, amongst a number of others. The act gave local authorities the right for the first time to define opening hours, and indeed gave them the right to ban the sale of alcohol completely within their boundaries. It was strengthened by the delightfully named 'Inebriates Act' of 1898, which made it illegal to supply alcohol to habitual drunks, and the 1902 Licensing Act added further restrictions – including the offence of being drunk in charge of a child – but did little to curb enthusiasm for enjoying the pleasures of a pint or more!

Despite the legislation, going to the pub remained a predominantly working-class activity well into the twentieth century, and one that remained largely the domain of the male. Working-class drinking to excess was widespread, and fuelled the growth of the temperance movement and the establishment of temperance hotels in every major holiday resort. The more affluent strata of society took their libations in gentlemen's clubs and, as these were 'private' rather than 'public' houses, they remained largely uncontrolled. Perhaps because of the social stigma attached, there are relatively few early photographs and photographic postcards of people drinking, but plenty of humorous cards drawing attention to the dangers of drink!

Left: 'Good Health' is one of a number of Edwardian postcards celebrating social drinking. Needless to say, the resurgent temperance movement did not approve of such postcards any more than it approved of licensed premises.

Opposite: Robert Richards (wearing the white apron), together with some customers and members of the local council, poses for photographer William Holiday on the occasion of the re-opening of the Harp Inn in Scholes, Wigan, on 8 May 1901. Just three weeks earlier, Richards had bought the 'Fully Licensed Public House known as the Harp Inn' at auction. The poster advertising the sale of the pub, eight cottages, three shops and a storeroom by auctioneer Mr George James Healy, is still attached to the side of the building.

A WALK IN THE GARDENS

The enjoyment of gardens is, of course, a long-established British tradition, and by the second half of Victoria's reign, the opportunity for visitors to enjoy the pleasures of nature's rich diversity was considerable. Botanical gardens and arboretums were to be found in many large cities, and public gardens in most towns.

Edinburgh's Royal Botanic Gardens, established in the seventeenth century, had moved to their present location at Inverleith in 1820. In 1858 the tallest palm house in Britain was opened there, and visitors flocked to see the rare plants from exotic parts of the world. Plant houses and formal gardens in other cities proved every bit as popular.

Charles Dickens Jnr noted in 1887 that, in Kensington Gardens, London, 'the collection of flowering trees along the north walk is in springtime almost worth a run up from the country to see.' Kew Gardens, which he described as 'among the most favourite resorts of the London holidaymaker, but have special value to the botanist and horticulturalist', was open free of charge every day of the week, morning and afternoon, except Sunday mornings, which were 'reserved for the necessary work of the gardeners, curators, and students.' Kew had been designated a 'National Botanical Garden' in 1840, and work on Decimus Burton's palm house, begun in 1844, was completed by 1848.

As the century drew to a close, Octavia Hill's interest in trying (sadly unsuccessfully) to save John Evelyn's garden at Sayes Court for posterity, eventually led to the formation of the National Trust, and the start of a highly successful programme of preservation, restoration and opening to the public of some of England's finest gardens.

Crowds entering the Municipal Gardens at Southport, seen here c.1908, enjoyed ornate floral gardens, a bandstand and concert arena, a tearoom, and elegant tree-lined avenues for promenaders.

Visitors in the newly opened pleasure gardens in Kirn near Dunoon on the Clyde coast, captured here in a photograph from 1904, present an almost tropical view.

For every garden open to the public, several dozen gardeners worked away behind the scenes in plant houses and in the gardens themselves. This view of Ipswich's Arboretum also dates from 1904.

Right: Two priests enjoying a quiet and contemplative walk in the well-manicured gardens of Stonyhurst College in Lancashire, in the autumn of 1858. The college, a Catholic boys school, and its environs were photographed extensively by Roger Fenton in 1858 and 1859.

Below: Visitors and gardeners pose for a photograph amidst the lush foliage and lupins at Brockwell Park Gardens, c.1906. On the back of the card, the sender wrote, 'This is a corner of the Park we go to often – the flowers are lovely in the old garden. It has been a gentleman's residence. There is all sorts of flowers, some tree fuches [sic] nearly as tall as I am, and lots of old fashioned flowers, hollyhocks, bur gomot [bergamot?] I cannot name a quarter of them.' The house and park – the former residence of John Blades, Esq in Lambeth – had been bought by London County Council in 1888, opened as a park in 1891, and expanded in 1899. Several fine postcard views of the gardens were available.

ROLLER SKATING

Although the use of wheeled skates can be traced back to the streets of Holland in the eighteenth century, roller skating as we know it today was introduced into America in 1863 using the four-wheeled skate invented by James Leonard Plimpton of New York, and quickly became a very popular pastime. It had crossed the Atlantic by the early 1870s, and in 1876, one William Bown of Birmingham patented a much-improved wheel design. In the following year, Joseph Henry Hughes, another Birmingham inventor, patented a further development using bearings to improve the smoothness of rotation (technology that later found many other applications).

'Rinking', as the sport was widely known, became the subject of a considerable number of humorous postcards; since falling over was seen as an unavoidable part of the experience, many of the cards show just that!

Rinks were opened in Norwich, London, Plymouth and elsewhere in Victorian times, some using concrete floors, while others used wood.

Top and middle: These two postcards from an extensive series published c.1904 are each made up from several different photographs, to create a collage of confusion on the rink!

Left: Entitled 'Some Funny Sights are Seen Here', this postcard, produced by Davidson Brothers of London, was posted from Earls Court in March 1909. It offers a good view of the four-wheeled skate that made the sport so popular.

An open tram taking a group of holidaymakers on a 'circular tour' of Blackpool, c.1910. These tramcars were known locally as the 'toast racks' because of their appearance when empty. Such tours were the precursors to the open-top bus tours offered in many towns and cities today. The particular view was available either as a sepia card, or the fully tinted version as seen here. Llandudno, Colwyn Bay and other resorts also operated tramcars of this design.

SIGHTSEEING

'Sight-seeing, in the opinion of many experienced travellers, is best avoided altogether', wrote Charles Dickens Jnr. 'It may well be, however, that this will be held to be a matter of opinion, and that sight-seeing will continue until the arrival of that traveller of Lord Macauley's, who has found his way into so many books and newspapers, but whose nationality shall not be hinted at here. One piece of advice to the intending sight-seer is at all events sound. Never go to see anything by yourself. If the show be a good one, you will enjoy yourself all the more in company; and the solitary contemplation of anything that is dull and tedious is one of the most depressing experiences of human life. Furthermore, an excellent principle – said to be of American origin – is never to enquire how far you may go, but to go straight on until you are told to stop. The enterprising sight-seer who proceeds on this plan, and who understands the virtue of "palm oil", and a calm demeanour, is sure to see anything he cares to see.'

Those words were written in 1887, and it would appear few heeded them – certainly as far as avoiding sightseeing is concerned. The Victorians and Edwardians developed a considerable appetite for the practice, embracing and enjoying guided tours just as much as individual exploration.

A group of holidaymakers enjoying the views from Fleetwood's Mount Pavilion, c.1906.

American holidaymakers on a sightseeing tour of London pose outside the Old Curiosity Shop in London's Portsmouth Street, made famous by Charles Dickens in the novel of the same name. Home to a waste paper merchant in 1908, today an antique shop occupies the site.

SHOPPING

During the closing years of Victoria's reign, the great shopping streets which still define our major cities were developed, and shopping moved, slowly but surely, from being a chore to being an enjoyable experience, and even a 'spectator sport'. During the nineteenth century, large sheets of plate glass – introduced in 1827 – replaced the traditional small panes in shop windows, as the purpose of the window changed from one of simply letting light into the interior, to being a means of enticing customers inside by displaying the shop's wares. At the same time, the majority of shops moved to a system of fixed prices, where earlier there had been a tradition of barter. As a result, potential customers walked from one shop to another – initially to compare products and prices, but eventually simply taking pleasure from admiring the clothes, shoes or other goods on display.

By the dawn of the twentieth century, being seen walking along the finest shopping streets had become as much a statement about one's status as promenading in parks and on the seafronts at major coastal resorts. In some fine streets – such as Edinburgh's Princes Street – the compliant promenading window shoppers accepted an unwritten code of conduct, which said that, when moving in one direction, they walked next to the window displays, while in the other direction they moved to the kerbside!

As late as 1887, Charles Dickens Jnr, in his *Dictionary of London*, wrote that London's Oxford Street 'ought to be the finest thoroughfare in the world. As a matter of fact it is not. It still contains houses which even in a third-rate street would be considered mean.' At that

Opposite top: James Valentine published this bustling view of Briggate in Leeds as a lantern slide in the 1870s; horse-drawn trams had been introduced in 1872.

Opposite: Shopping as a spectator sport – a group of tourists watch as fishwives on the beach at Seaton in East Lothian sell their wares in 1904.

Below: Manchester's Deansgate was already an established shopping street, with large department stores lining both sides by the time this 1902 photograph was taken. Judging by the number of notices in the windows, and the crowd of shoppers in the doorway, the large store to the right of the open-topped tram was having a sale!

time, 'window shopping' was in its infancy and Dickens noted that even on Regent Street, 'although some of the handsomest and most attractive shops, even in this street of tradesmen's palaces, are on the western side, it is comparatively deserted by passengers.' But by that time, habits were changing, and within a very few years, the side of the street lined with 'tradesmen's palaces' would be the busier side! Improved public transport, and an increasingly affluent middle class in the Edwardian era, changed shopping and window shopping to a pleasant and social leisure pastime.

Britain's – and possibly the world's – first department store, Bainbridge's in Newcastle, opened in 1838 as a drapery and fashion shop. By 1859, the range of goods had expanded hugely, and the store adopted a policy of accounting by separate departments (three years before Le Bon Marché, France's claimant to be the first, did the same). The Newcastle store, part of John Lewis since 1952, changed its name in 2002 after 160 years!

A LIFE ON THE OCEAN WAVE

Crossing the Atlantic was an experience enjoyed by the wealthy, and endured by the poor. The conditions under which both lived during the crossing were as far removed from each other as might be possible.

For the steerage passengers, the crossing was something which had to be endured if the promise of the 'New World' was to be realised, but for the wealthy, the crossing to or from America was one of life's many pleasures.

Entertainment was lavish and, when the weather was fine, organised deck games were the order of the day. If the weather was poor, covered promenade decks enabled daily strolls to be taken without being buffeted by the often ferocious Atlantic weather.

On other seas and oceans, the experience was much the same. One traveller, Mary Garnett, on a voyage through the Mediterranean to Egypt in February 1890, wrote in her diary that life on board included 'promenading, playing quoits, skipping with skipping ropes held by two… Last evening we had charades in the dining saloon. The vessel was steady enough to allow one to distinguish sounds, for the previous night had been only 'a crash of matter', and myself a shuttle-cock tossed upon my bed like a battledore… A dance on deck tonight; the young folks did fly about and enjoy themselves, but Miss Hunter, being of a serious turn of mind, remarked that "you could not have got them to take as much exercise for a good object!"' As far as the young are concerned, some things never change!

Cruising started to gain popularity during the Edwardian years, with Cunard one of the first to cater for this new market – albeit originally for wealthy American visitors to Europe – diverting the newly-built RMS *Caronia* from trans-Atlantic service to Mediterranean cruising in 1906.

Opposite top: A group of passengers enjoying a game of deck quoits on board a liner in 1908. Despite postcards like this having been produced in considerable numbers to promote cruising, they remain relatively scarce.

Above: 'This is how we go ashore', wrote 'Auntie' to her niece, Miss F. Mansion, in August 1908. As many foreign harbours could not accommodate the larger vessels that were being brought into service on long voyages, transferring to a smaller tender was the only way of disembarking. The wicker basket could hold two passengers at a time, so being winched over from the liner to the tender would never have been a speedy undertaking, and in choppy seas, probably anything but a pleasant one! This postcard was posted to Cranbrook in Kent from the South African port of East London.

Above: Princes Street, Edinburgh in 1896, with Thomas Cook's Travel Office at the end of the gardens.

Below: Visitors to Rome in the 1870s could buy an extensive range of photographic mementoes of their experience. This view of St Peter's Square was taken during an Easter Sunday Mass, c. 1875.

Opposite: At the Rigi Mountain Railway in Switzerland, a popular visitor location since the 1860s, visitors throughout the Victorian and Edwardian era could select from a catalogue of regularly updated images. This coloured 'Photochrome' view dates from c. 1896.

HOLIDAYING ABROAD

The Victorian Grand Tours of Europe and of the Middle East were as much about advertising your status as they were about the experience of travel. As travel became easier, and the middle classes became more affluent, travel to mainland Europe, and later farther afield, became increasingly popular. As the numbers increased, so did the availability of every tourist need – accommodation, guides, interpreters, guidebooks and photographic mementoes. Thomas Cook organised his first trips to France in the early 1850s, and by the end of the decade his catalogue of tours offered the opportunity to travel much further afield.

In the 1850s and 1860s, travelling conditions were pretty primitive – ships were small, so the channel crossing to France was often difficult, and journeys to the Mediterranean through the Bay of Biscay could be really unpleasant. But still they went!

The diaries of four Cheshire travellers, the Garnetts and the Marsdens, recall two 'tours' in the 1880s and 1890s. While Mrs Garnett wrote a daily diary, and Mr Garnett sketched wherever they travelled, the Marsdens collected together a photographic account of their experiences.

There was the constant fear of any number of diseases – which Mrs Garnett felt could be caught just by walking down any foreign street – and finally there was the great unforgivable characteristic of the 'natives' wherever they went: they were all foreign, and unable in most cases to understand even the basic rudiments of English! Settled into a high-class hotel where English was spoken, and pens and writing paper were freely available for the guests, Mrs Garnett wrote in her diary of a Nile trip with several overnight stopovers, 'We have been such

vagabonds upon the face of the earth, sleeping in such a variety of hotels (and such wretched berths on the *Chuzan*), and having been addressed in so many different languages, that now we really seem to have found a resting place and a home.'

The beauties of the Nile were undeniable, and apparent even to first-time travellers – the little booklets which Thomas Cook's tourists took with them not only told them so, but also told them how to respond to what they saw – and the ruined temples and carvings impressed the two families from Warrington. What made the greatest mark on them all, however, was their visit to Giza and the ascent of the Great Pyramid of Cheops.

The view from the top of the great pyramid was the high spot – quite literally – of the tour, but getting there was the most fraught part of the whole journey. Mary Garnett's diary recounts all her fears and misgivings about the whole project: 'A visit to the Pyramids means a hand-to-hand fight with dragomans, rightly named. I had twelve to myself, who badgered me to buy scarabs which I knew had been made in Birmingham, and to haul me up the stony structure against my will and finally haul me into the interior... for once in their clutches you would not leave those dark and dreadful recesses while a single coin remained in your pocket.' Remember, this is a holiday she is writing about!

Later in her diaries, recounting the second trip (one wonders why she went back if she disliked it so much), Mary Garnett describes 'Lily M's' first encounter with the Pyramid and the ever-present dragoman. 'We drove to the Pyramids of Gizeh yesterday, and Lily and Mr H. M. were lugged up. Had about four Arabs each. I watched the operation through my glass, and when some distance from the top, perceived that Lily's party stopped and all the Arabs crowded down. I feared she had fainted. The heat was intense and she had gone off in a faint at the tombs of Beni Hassan after a great climb... At last they rose and went forward... When she came down, she told me she had sat down to rest, and had been showing those men the photographs of all her friends and Sunday School scholars, which she was carrying to the top! She is not the least afraid of the men, and even poor I, yesterday, did not suffer as I did last time, for I made them know I had been last year and knew all about it.'

The picture of the ascent of the pyramid is an eloquent statement about the social and personal challenges that went with the experience. There are, of course, more servants than travellers and in that respect, the relationships are as one might expect. But there is much more to the picture. At the base of the pyramid, all is normal. The travellers are seated on camels; the servants are on foot. The male travellers are engaging with the camera, not with the servants; the female travellers are looking out of shot, not relating to anything that was going on except, perhaps, their ever-present fear of the dragoman, the Arab. As soon as the ascent of the pyramid commences, however, relying on the Egyptian guides became essential. Ascent of the huge stone blocks in what passed for holiday attire could not easily be achieved without strong Arab arms to haul the visitors up. And for British ladies to hold hands with the Arabs they so feared... well, some things just had to be endured!

Opposite: The ascent of the Pyramid of Cheops, Giza, Egypt, photographed by the Zangaki Brothers in the 1870s. An eloquent and highly informative take on the challenges of undertaking the Middle Eastern Grand Tour.

INDEX

Aberdeen 34
Aberystwyth 42
Abraham Brothers 88, 90–1
Accrington Football Club 39
Alexandra Palace 89
All England Croquet & Lawn tennis Club 107
Alpine Club of London 90
Ascot 22, 24
Aston Villa Football Club 39
Automobile Club 100
Baden-Powell, Lord Robert 41
Baldry, William 93
Bannantyne 104–5
Bean, Alderman George 68
Bexhill-on-Sea 100
Birnbeck Pier, 69
Blackburn Rovers FC 40
Blackpool 12, 16–17, 68–9, 118
Blatchford, Robert 101
Blyth 4
Bolton Wanderers FC 40
Bournemouth 14, 78–9
Brighton 14
Brockwell Park 116
Brooklands 100
Brownsea Island 41
Burnham on Sea 50–1, 82
Burnley Football Club 39
Bury St Edmund 84–5
Bute 94
Caitlin's Royal Pierrots 42
Campbell, S.A. 74
Carnoustie 35
Chester 25, 106
Chic 24
Chislehurst Golf Club 34
Clacton on Sea 43, 45, 47, 74–5, 77, 79, 107
Clarion Cycling Club 101
Clarion, The 101
Cleethorpes 81
Climbing in the English Lake District 91
Codman, Richard 31
Coleridge, Samuel Taylor 90
Compleat Angler, The 65
Coney Island 69
Cook, Thomas 9, 86, 124–5, 127
Corinthians Football Club 40
Crieff Golf Club 37
Crystal Palace 7–8, 69, 89, 96–7
Derby County Football Club 40
De La Warr, Earl 100
Dickens, Charles 45, 119
Dickens, Charles Jnr. 19, 23, 27, 30, 33, 52, 56, 89, 112, 114, 118, 120–1
Dickens's *Dictionary of London* 23, 27, 30, 33, 52, 56, 89, 112, 114, 118, 120–1
Dickens's *Dictionary of the Thames* 19
Dewsbury 54
Doncaster 22–24
Dunoon 115
Earle, Godwynne 83
Earls Court 117
East London (South Africa) 123
Eccleston Ferry 106
Edinburgh 34
Epsom Racecourse 25
Ettrick Bay 94
Evelyn, John 114
Everton Football Club 40
Exemouth 108–9
Exposition Universelle, Paris 9
Farndale Hunt 60
Fenton, Roger 10, 32–3, 84, 116
Field, The 19
Finsbury Park 53
Flamborough headf 92
Fleetwood 8–9, 119

Football Association 39
Football League 39
Franco-British Exhibition 1908 8, 99
Frith, Francis 86
Gairloch 104
Garnet, Mary 122, 125–7
Garswood Hall 89
Gilsland 72
Girl Guides 41
Glasgow 66, 104
Goring 102
Gorleston-on-Sea 84–5
Grasmere 93
Great Exhibition 7, 97
Great Yarmouth 50–1, 79–80
Guide to the Lakes 88
Hall, Hepple 112
Hampstead Heath 17
Hampton Court 89
Handforth 101
Harrogate 95
Harry Frewin's 'White Coons' 43
Hartmann & Company 15
Henley on Thames 18–19, 20–1
Hermann, Vincent 100
Hill, Octavia 58, 114
Hoylake 35
Hughes, Joseph Henry 117
Hunsdonbury Cricket Club 33
Hunter, Sir Robert 58
Hythe 106
Inebriates Act 1898 113
International Exhibition 1862 97
Intoxicating Liquor (Licensing) Bill 1872 112
Ipswich 115
Isle of Arran 54
Japan-British Exhibition 1910 99
Jones, O.G. 91
Kensington Gardens 114
Keswick 88, 90
Kew Gardens 114
Kirkcaldy 15
Kirn 115
Kyles of Bute 104–5
Lake District 86–8
Lamlash 37, 54
Landseer, Sir Edwin 62
Lang, Andrew 65
Leith 55, 77
Licensing Acts 112–13
Liverpool 31
Llandudno 31, 43, 48
Loch Katrine 74–5, 103–4
London 15, 77, 116, 119
London Labour and the London Poor 31
London Regents Park Zoo 26–30
London Stereoscopic & Photographic Company 7, 16–17
Lowestoft 18–19
Mablethorpe 42, 44
Maidenhead 102–3
Manchester 71, 120
Manchester Ship Canal 77
Margate 44, 81
Marylebone Cricket Club 33
Maxim, Sir Hiram 69
Maxim's Flying Machines 68–9
Mayhew, Henry 31
Mayson, Henry 93
Minerva cars 100
Morecambe 61
Morley, Ebenezer Cob 39
Morris, 'Old' Tom 35
Musselburgh 34
Napier cars 100
National Trust, the 114
Negretti & Zambra 97
New Brighton 45
Newcastle United Football Club 39

North British Railway 98
Nottingham Goose Fair 70
Notts County Football Club 39–40
Ogle, Thomas 86
Oldham 70–1
Olympic Games 98
Oval, The 33
Oxford 18, 71
PS *Gareloch* 77
PS *Ivanhoe* 77
PS *Koh-i-Noor* 74–5
PS *Royal Sovereign* 76–7
PS *Suffolk* 74–5
PS *Wemyss Castle* 77
Philadelphia 69
Photochrome Company of Zurich 105
Plimpton, James Leonard 117
Plymouth 48
Portobello 48–49
Preston North End Football Club 40
Raffles, Sir Stamford 27
Ramsgate 46–7
Rawnsley, Canon Hardwicke 58
RMS Caronia 122
Robertson, Allan 35
Rosedale 60
Royal Blackheath Golf Club 34
Royal Botanic Gardens Edinburgh 114
Royal Liverpool Golf Club 35
Russell, Earl Francis, 83
Ryanair 69
Saughton Hall, Edinburgh 98–9
Scafell 90
Scafell Pike 91
Scarborough 44
Scouting for Boys 41
Seaton 120
Shaftesbury, Lord 112
Sheffield FC 39
Shurey's Publications 23, 64
Skegness 36
Southend-on-Sea 66
Southport 17, 47, 69, 79–80, 95, 114
Southsea 51
St Andrews 34
St Leger, the 22–24
Steadman, George 93
SS Rob Roy 75, 103
SS Sir Walter Scott 75
Stereoscopic Magazine 7
Stoke Football Club 40
Stonyhurst College 116
Sunderland Football Club 39
Teddington 102–3
Trossachs 74–5, 86
Tuck, Raphael 62–3, 64
Twain, Mark 34
Ullswater 86
Valentine & Company 56, 120
Victoria (Queen) 73, 103
Wakes Week 70–1
Walton, Izaac 64–5
West, Thomas 88
West Bromwich Albion Football Club 40
Weston-super-Mare 67, 69
Weymouth 83
Wilson, G.W. 64, 86
Wimbledon 34
Windermere 87
Wolverhampton Wanderers Football Club 40
Wordsworth, William 34
White City 8, 97–99
Wigan 6, 71, 112–113
Wigan Pier 74
Zangaki Brothers 127
Zoological Society 30